ENOUGH IS ENOUGH

Fintan O'Toole is one of Ireland's most respected and contro-versial political and cultural commentators, and an acclaimed biographer and critic. His books include *White Savage*, *A Traitor's Kiss* and *Ship of Fools*, which was a Number One bestseller in Ireland. He lives in Dublin and is a columnist for the *Irish Times*.

Enough is Enough

How to Build a New Republic

FINTAN O'TOOLE

faber and faber

First published in 2010
by Faber and Faber Ltd
Bloomsbury House
74–77 Great Russell Street
London WC1B 3DA

Typeset by Faber and Faber Ltd
Printed in England by CPI Mackays, Chatham
All rights reserved
© Fintan O'Toole, 2010

The right of Fintan O'Toole to be identified as author
of this work has been asserted in accordance with Section 77
of the Copyright, Designs and Patents Act 1988

A CIP record for this book
is available from the British Library

ISBN 978–0–571–27008–8

2 4 6 8 10 9 7 5 3 1

to Sam, Fionn and the future

Contents

Acknowledgements

I had not intended to write this book. Its origins lie in public responses to a book I wrote in 2009 – *Ship of Fools: How Stupidity and Corruption Sank the Celtic Tiger*. That polemical analysis of the factors that led to the destruction of Irish prosperity made readers angry – or perhaps it merely plugged in to an existing rage. In public readings and discussions, however, the expressions of fury, bewilderment and alienation inevitably led on to a single question – what do we do next?

I do not pretend to have anything like a full answer to that question. It did strike me, however, that it would be irresponsible to stir up anger and then walk away from the consequences. The discussions were marked, to a surprisingly large extent, by their avoidance of mere furious venting. The people I encountered were thoughtful, engaged and hungry for ideas. Whether or not this book adequately feeds that hunger, it owes its existence to them and I thank them for it.

The chapter 'The Myth of the Republic' expands on an essay first written for an RTE Thomas Davis lecture; I am grateful to the editor of that series, Mary Jones, for her inspiration. I am extremely grateful to everyone at Faber and Faber for their extraordinary efforts in making a book like this possible. Polemical interventions in a fluid political and economic crisis are not the normal business of one of the world's great literary publishers. I am indebted to my editor Neil Belton for his unflinching support and to Charles Boyle and Kate Murray-Browne for their grace under pressure.

My thanks, too, to my agent Derek Johns, and to Geraldine Kennedy and my colleagues at the *Irish Times* for tolerating my absences and preoccupations. My love, as ever, to Clare Connell, and to Samuel and Fionn.

'Stupidity is doing the same things
and expecting different results'
– Roy Keane

The Wrong Map

During the vicious fighting in the Alps between the Italians and the Austro-Hungarian Empire, an inexperienced young lieutenant is sent out on a reconnaissance mission with a small detachment under his command. He leads them high into the Alps until they are overtaken by a dreadful snow-storm. The blizzards will not abate. The men can barely see in front of them, and even if they could see, all paths and landmarks have been obliterated by the snow.

At night they huddle in a crevasse. In the morning, there is nothing but snow and ice, nothing by which they can take their bearings. Frozen and dazed, the lieutenant leads the men across the wastes, with no idea where they are going. After the second night they wake to more snow. Freezing, exhausted, and in despair, they lie there waiting for death.

From a corner of his numbed brain, the lieutenant drags out the memory of a map. He searches in his knapsack and finds it. As he spreads it out in front of him, he begins to rec-ognise the contours of the mountains, the ravines and gullies, the peaks and troughs of this region of the Alps. He becomes calm and focused. He stands up and addresses the men for the first time with confidence. He tells them that they are safe, that he has got his bearings and will lead them back to camp. They somehow get to their feet and follow him as he plots their descent, reading his compass and tracing the delicate lines of the map.

After three days and much suffering, they make it back to camp. The captain who sent them out had been racked with guilt for leaving these men under the command of a neophyte. He has given them up for dead. When he sees them limp home, he is overjoyed. He asks the lieutenant to tell him what happened: 'We were overtaken by the blizzard; we lost the paths; we wandered in despair; we froze; we gave ourselves up for dead. And then I remembered that, of course, I had a map. I realised that I could match the lines on the paper to the contours I was seeing all around me. I knew the way home. The men began to believe in me. We plotted our course and here we are.'

The captain is thrilled with the story and asks to see the map. The lieutenant fishes it out of his knapsack and spreads it out before them. It is, the captain notices, a map not of the Alps but of the Pyrenees.

This story, told by the Czech poet Miroslav Holub, is not a bad parable for contemporary Ireland. We are beset by a blizzard of woes, the paths have been obscured and we are in despair. We need a map. The map will probably be wrong, but it might nonetheless give us something to follow and it might help us to get home. This book is offered, very modestly, as just such a map. It is almost certainly wrong – no one in the midst of Ireland's current crisis can say anything with great confidence about the next five years, never mind the longer-term future. But there is no other map: there are few peacetime precedents anywhere for Ireland's current predicament. Very few developed economies have ever contracted as quickly and as sharply as the Irish one did in 2008 and 2010. (GNP has fallen by around 13 per cent.) Very few banking crises have ever been as severe as Ireland's. And no developed society since the Second World War has faced to quite the same extent Ireland's combination of an internally generated crisis of these proportions and an external global crisis in which financial, environmental, economic and political uncertainties run so deep.

Mapping Ireland's future is even more difficult because so many of the old landmarks have disappeared. The twin towers of southern Irish identity – Catholicism and nationalism – were already teetering before the great boom began in 1995. Institutional Catholicism began to lose its grip in the 1960s; by the early 1990s its foundations were already undermined by secularisation, the sexual revolution and its own scandals. Nationalism had become vastly more complicated, a set of troubling questions rather than of easy answers. The vicious conflict in Northern Ireland, the venality of 'patriotic' politicians, the effects of membership of the European Union, and cultural globalisation all made nationalism a slippery and ambiguous concept.

This, indeed, is the reason why the Celtic Tiger was embraced with such fervour and why its sudden demise has been a psychic, as well as an economic, shock. Booms always engender hysteria, but what made the Irish one so extreme was that it was filling a void. The Celtic Tiger wasn't just an economic ideology. It was also a substitute identity. It was a new way of being that arrived just at the point when Catholicism and nationalism were not working any more. At its cheapest, this identity expressed itself in a mad consumerism, in an arrogance towards the rest of the world, in a wilful refusal of all ties of history and tradition. But there were other things wrapped up in it too – optimism, confidence, a new openness and ease, an absence of fear. The banking collapse of 2008 didn't just kill off the arrogance and acquisitive mania, it also swept away the hopefulness and the sense of possibility. It is not just money that has been lost; it is a sense of what, for better and worse, it meant to be 'us'.

There is now the uneasy feeling of going back to the past, but without the comforts that the past contained. On the one hand, there is no going back to the institutional Catholicism or the nationalism that emerged so powerfully – and so much in tandem – in the nineteenth century. An *Irish Times* poll in September 2010 found that just 13 per cent of respondents described themselves as 'strongly religious' – the same proportion as described themselves as being 'not religious at all'. Among the young, the drift away from a powerful religious identity is even more pronounced. Of those aged between 18 and 24, just 4 per cent are 'strongly religious', compared to 22 per cent who are 'not religious at all'. Among those aged between 25 and 34, the figures are 6 per cent and 16 per cent respectively. And the cities now have levels of religious practice that would have been unimaginable before the Celtic Tiger. Sixty-two per cent of all urban respondents reported attending religious services 'only occasionally' or 'never'. The children of the boom years pray to different gods.

The same goes for nationalism. Asked to rank, in the same poll, 'issues of concern' in terms of their importance, just 2 per cent put 'the reunification of Ireland' first, and 71 per cent put it last in a list of seven options. To put that 2 per cent in context, it is the same proportion as those who, given a list of seven major issues, simply answered 'don't know'. The strong nationalists are now as numerous as those who have no opinions at all. Hardly anyone now takes comfort in the idea that a United Ireland would solve all the problems. In the 1980s Fianna Fáil's don, Charles Haughey, could still use nationalist rhetoric to some effect as a way of taking people's minds off economic collapse and political corruption. That rhetoric doesn't work as an effective distraction any more, let alone as a collective binding force.

The disappearance of these landmarks does not mean, how-ever, that Ireland faces into the current crisis with a psychic clean sheet. On the contrary there is a powerful – and power-fully disturbing – return of the repressed. For all its failures and insanities, the boom did liberate the Irish from the sense of history as, in James Joyce's formulation, 'a nightmare from which I am trying to awake'. It banished the underlying Irish sense of doom, the bitter spectre of self-contempt that was always whispering in our ears that we would screw it all up. And then we screwed it all up. Given unimaginable bounty – a durable peace settlement, overflowing state cof-fers, a generation born into the expectation of limitless pos-sibilities – we managed not just to squander it but to end up in some respects worse off than we were before. The question that nags at us now is: if we couldn't make a go of it in the longest boom in our history, how can we make a go of it with a vast burden of debt, a continuing global crisis and a landscape scarred with half-built houses whose increasingly decrepit emptiness mocks our delusions of grandeur?

The sense of returning to the well-worn path of failure is not abstract. It is embodied in a deep-seated national reflex – emigration. A huge part of the old, pre-boom notion of what it meant to be Irish was the knowledge of belonging to a migratory culture. That culture seemed not simply to die out in the boom years but to be turned on its head: Ireland became a place of immigration rather than emigration. In the aftermath of the boom, the old pattern began to reassert it-self. First, many of the new immigrants left. Then Irish-born people began to leave too. In the year to April 2010 there was net outward migration of 34,500 – the highest level since 1989.

With the rate of emigration highly likely to have increased since then, there is every chance that the overall Irish population will have decreased by the time of the 2011 census. Given that the most profound effect of the boom was a steady increase in the number of people living in the Republic – an achievement that seemed to mark the end of Ireland's long period as the great anomaly among developed societies – this will be a depressing turn of the wheel of historical fortune.

There is, then, a feeling of going back to the past, but without the comforts of religion and the certainties of national destiny that made past failures bearable. It is not, after all, so surprising that the collective response to the crisis has been relatively passive. There is both hot anger and cold fury, but these emotions are almost crowded out by a host of other feelings. There is deep despair – a sense of futility and fatalism. There is self-contempt – what could you expect from this bloody country? There is fear – unlike previous Irish busts, the majority of people have a great deal to lose. There is the feeling of being buried beneath a mountain of debt – both personal and collective. And above all there is shock and disorientation, the feeling of being caught in an exposed place in a blinding snowstorm of woes, under the command of clueless leaders, without a map.

Where do we begin to rummage for a map? In the despair. To steal a line from the playwright Tom Murphy, 'it is from this dark area, this rising darkness of our despair that the solution is to derive'.[1] In a sense, Ireland needs to despair thoroughly and comprehensively. It needs to lose every last vestige of hope in the whole governing culture. It has to rec-ognise that the hole is very deep and that the frantic shovelling of the ruling elite is not the digging of an escape tunnel. It is merely the widening of the hole.

There was never much chance that the elite that created the catastrophe would be able to resolve it. What was hard to reckon was just how much worse they could make it. The principal response of the government has been what is almost certainly, in proportional terms, the most expensive bank bailout in history, and it has been an almost complete failure.

A month after the government decided, in September 2008, to guarantee all the liabilities of the Irish banks including Anglo Irish Bank and Irish Nationwide Building Society, both of which had been no more than casinos for property developers, the Minister for Finance Brian Lenihan boasted that the Irish rescue plan would be 'the cheapest bailout in the world so far'. He contrasted his cunning scheme with the reaction of governments in the UK and US, where 'billions and billions of taxpayers' money are being poured into financial institutions'. The crisis, he suggested, was all but over and his plan would 'guarantee to the wider economy the necessary lifeblood that the system requires'.[2] Irish people were thus being told two things: that the bank rescue package would be uniquely cheap, certainly not amounting to 'billions and billions of taxpayers' money', and that within a short period the plan would have ensured that credit was flowing again into the Irish economy.

If the government actually believed these things, it was making the biggest miscalculation since Napoleon decided that he could waltz all the way to Moscow. But it is not at all clear that the government did believe its own line, even in the early days of the rescue plan. It was obvious to the most casual observer that Anglo and Nationwide were toxic institutions whose standards of governance had been appalling and whose operations had been fuelled by hysterical recklessness. The idea that such institutions could be rescued cheaply was at best delusional, at worst a deliberate attempt to hide the scale of the crisis from the public. And the notion that nationalising the debts of Anglo and Nationwide would lead to a flow of credit to the real economy was ridiculous. These institutions had never never lent significant sums to the real economy outside of their own bubble of hyperactive property developers; any assumption that they would start doing so when they were grotesquely insolvent was patent nonsense.

It is hard to say exactly what the government thought it was doing in tying the fate of the state to that of Anglo Irish Bank, because the explanations kept changing as the black hole sucked in more and more public money.

The Irish people were given, in all, five different explanations by the government of why they should continue to pour money into Anglo and its mini-me Irish Nationwide. The first was that these institutions were basically sound but needed temporary rescue from a liquidity crisis. No one now needs to be told how stupid that was, and it is hard to believe that even at the time this is what the government itself thought. On the day the government guaranteed Anglo's debts, the bank's bosses had earlier gone to Bank of Ireland, asking it to take them over because they were insolvent.

The second explanation was the need to give Anglo money in order to get credit flowing into the economy again. This was always a cynical line spun for the supposedly gullible masses – but it took almost two years before the government actually admitted that Anglo would never lend money into the economy again.

The third reason was that it was vital to avoid having zombie banks. This actually has been achieved – as the *Financial Times* pointed out two years after the guarantee, Anglo is nothing as lively as a zombie. It's a 'rotting corpse'.

The fourth proposition was that saving Anglo and Nationwide was necessary to maintain Ireland's 'credibility' with the international financial markets. In fact, watching a state borrow €30 billion at ruinously high interest rates in order to shovel them into a grave merely enhanced Ireland's incredibility on the financial markets. By associating Irish sovereign debt with Anglo's bottomless pit of losses, the government merely succeeded in driving up the costs of state borrowing to unsustainable levels. By late September 2010 the interest rate that Ireland had to offer in order to entice investors to buy government bonds was three times that offered by Germany.

The only excuse for the immense waste of public money on Anglo that made any sense was the last one: that the European Union, and more specifically the European Central Bank, had decided that no European bank should be allowed to fail. This would have been all very well – if the government had gone to the EU and ECB and negotiated a deal whereby they would share the cost of making sure that Anglo did not go down. Instead, in what seemed like a demented determination to save face at all costs, the government assumed, on behalf of the Irish people, the burden of saving the honour of European banking.

The direct cost of this was staggering. Official figures put the best-case scenario at €45 billion and the worst at €50 billion. Of this €50 billion, almost €40 billlion – €34.4 billon for Anglo and €5.4 billion for Irish Nationwide – is completely dead money. There is zero chance of a return and no economic benefit. But even this may be an understatement. In August 2010 Standard and Poor's put the full cumulative total cost of bailing out the Irish banks at €90 billion.

Implicit in this is that there will be many years of austerity, with continuing cuts in basic social services. Financial strategists Simon Johnson and Peter Boone, writing in the *New York Times*, estimated that 'the debts of Irish banks could easily result in a charge to government debt equal to one-third of GNP'. They added that 'Under the current program, we estimate that each Irish family of four will be liable for €200,000 in public debt by 2015. There are only 73,000 children born into the country each year, and these children will be paying off debts for decades to come — as well as needing to accept much greater austerity than has already been put into force. There is no doubt that social welfare systems, health care and education spending will decline sharply.'[3]

Similarly, Wolfgang Munchau wrote in the *Financial Times*:

> The Irish government massively underestimated the scale of the problem in its banking sector. On my own back-of-the-envelope calculations, the cost of a financial sector bail-out may exceed 30 per cent of Irish gross domestic product, if you make realistic assumptions about bad debt write-offs and apply a conservative trajectory for future economic growth. We know from economic history that countries enter into longish phases of stagnation after a financial crisis. Ireland suffered an extreme crisis. In the light of what we know, the safe assumption to make for Ireland . . . is that there will not be much nominal growth in the next five years.[4]

But while international experts were drawing these grim conclusions, the Irish elite invented a word for all of this pain – manageable. It was the favourite term in the lexicon of the government, the Central Bank, the business and employers' organisations and those in the media who continue to cling on to their faith in the old orthodoxies.

There are three simple questions about the notion that the bailout is 'manageable'. The first is about numbers. How can you decide that a cost is manageable when you don't know what that cost is? To take Anglo Irish Bank alone, the estimates for the likely final costs ranged, over less than two years, from zero to €4 billion to a worst-case of €40 billion. Even in September 2010 the sums given to the taxpayer by official sources were somewhere between €25 billion and €40 billion. That's a spread of €15 billion. The implication is that a figure like this has no effect on the manageability of the crisis. So, if €40 billion is manageable, €54 billion would be equally manageable, and so on. The government and its allies declared every new (and inevitably higher) estimate of the cost to be one with which the country could cope. By this logic, there was no cost that would be unmanageable.

Secondly, if the government's approach is perfectly manageable, why is it unique in history? Never since modern national banking systems emerged in the eighteenth century has any government spent such a large proportion of national income cleaning up after a banking collapse. And this cost feeds into a larger deficit that is itself unique: 32 per cent in 2010, ten times the maximum permitted in the eurozone. There is no example of any developed country running a deficit of this size in peacetime.

The deficit for 2010, including the banking costs, is higher as a proportion of GDP than that incurred by the United

States at the height of the Second World War. Optimists may point out that the current banking costs are temporary. So was the Second World War.

How come nobody else, in the history of the world, has come up with the idea that spending on this scale for no tangible economic return is acceptable? For the Irish political and financial elite to be right on this one, they have to have discovered a wisdom that has eluded all governments, administrators and economists for the past four centuries. Given that they constitute almost entirely the same set of people who created the catastrophe in the first place, the chances of this being the case seem less than good.

Thirdly, manageable for whom? It is undoubtedly the case that a lot of people will be able to manage just fine as social services contract, poverty increases and unemployment soars. The entire political, administrative, banking and commenting elite will be among the managers. But is it manageable for the Down's syndrome child who turns up in school to find that her special needs assistant isn't there anymore? Is it manageable for the 85-year-old man who's being discharged from hospital into the care of his 90-year-old wife? Is it manageable for the couple who have a €400,000 mortgage on a house worth €250,000 and who have just lost their jobs? Or for the 5,000 people who are already living on the streets?

What the great and the good really mean when they use the word is not that the financial fallout is manageable. It is that the people are manageable. The assumption is that you can squeeze health and education, do almost nothing to create jobs, lock the economy into a downward spiral of cuts and depression, and there will be no long-term political or social consequence. Underpinning all the gambles on the banks is the ultimate gamble – on the infinite masochism and/or gullibility of the Irish people.

Which brings us back to the heart of the matter – politics. In *Ship of Fools* I argued that the collapse of the Irish economy was rooted not primarily in banking or property development or the lack of regulation, but in the political culture that created a lethal cocktail of all of these elements. If this is true – and the point has not been contradicted – it follows that there is no way out of the current crisis that does not have, at its very core, a radical transformation of the existing political culture. The purpose of this book is to provide a rough map of how that transformation can take place.

Politics is at the centre of the basic assumption on which the current official strategy is based: there is a calculated judgement that the Irish people will take all the pain of shrinking public services, mass unemployment and forced emigration in order to pay off the gambling debts of their betters and that Ireland will remain politically stable. The judgement is that all of this can be done and that at the distant end of the process there will still be a functioning democratic society in place in Ireland. There will still be an 'us' that includes both those who ran up the debts and those who have to pay them off.

Paradoxically, while politics is thus central to the strategy, the one thing that cannot be discussed in relation to the bank bailout is its politics. The governing elite has woven a retrospective narrative to explain how Ireland got to be where it is. It identified the villains – the reckless bankers, the feckless regulators, the delusional developers. But what absolutely cannot be mentioned is the nexus in which all of this happened, the political culture whose shorthand name is Fianna Fáil.

It is crucial to bear in mind that there has been no attempt to deal with – or even to acknowledge – the toxic nature of the intertwining of politics and banking, and thus no move to destroy the political culture that led to the crash. The official narrative of the making of the crisis, contained in the report of the new governor of the Central Bank, Patrick Honohan, is notably evasive on one of the key questions – political and governmental collusion with the bankers. 'Evasive' is not the right word; 'tortured', 'twisted' or 'tormented' might be more accurate.

Firstly, Honohan notes 'the suggestion by some commentators that the fact that some banking personages were politically well connected might have been a key factor in discouraging aggressive supervisory intervention'.[5] He then tenders a weirdly inconclusive conclusion: 'None of the persons interviewed during the investigation agreed with this proposition, with several noting (rightly) that it was quite predictable that senior banking figures would have political contacts. While it is easy to imagine that senior management or [Central Bank/Financial Services Authority] Board or Authority Members might have instinctively and almost unconsciously shied away from aggressive action to restrain politically connected bankers and developers during a runaway property boom, no evidence has been presented suggesting that this was the case.' The question that screams out for an answer is why, exactly, is it 'easy to imagine' in Ireland that the top regulatory brass would instinctively shy away from taking on 'politically connected bankers and developers'?

Even more weirdly, however, Honohan confines to a footnote a set of statements about Anglo Irish Bank and Irish Nationwide Building Society (INBS) that seem at once to acknowledge the political connections to Fianna Fáil of their bosses, Seán FitzPatrick and Michael Fingleton, and to dismiss the significance of those connections:

> Although it became quite clear to top Financial Regulator decision-makers that senior Anglo figures were well-liked in political circles, and it cannot be excluded that this played a part in their subsequent continuation in office for some months after September [2008, when the banks almost collapsed and the government had to step in], there was, until very late in the day, no perceived need to take regulatory action against them. The central management figure in INBS [Fingleton] was seen as an overly dominating figure that needed to be surrounded by a stronger governance structure. While it was understood by all that he was politically well-connected, the failure to resolve the issue is not attributed by anyone involved to his having a privileged status. While unconscious factors may have been at work, FR management and directors agree that there is no evidence of political representations being made on his behalf aimed at influencing regulatory decisions.

This is the sum total of official accounting for the Fianna Fáil factor in the whole debacle. How did the regulators come to know that Seán FitzPatrick and his sidekicks at Anglo were 'well-liked in political circles'? How did they know that Michael Fingleton was 'politically well-connected'? What 'unconscious factors' were at work? Nobody, least of all the public that has ended up paying the price, needs to know.

Most important of all, Honohan rather pointedly avoids the big question. This is not whether the regulators were influenced by their knowledge of the political connections to Fianna Fáil of the likes of FitzPatrick and Fingleton. (Given the general and deliberate timidity of the regulators, one would have to ask, as Dorothy Parker asked of the death of Calvin Coolidge, 'How could they tell?') It is whether the government itself, in its crucial decision in September 2008, was influenced by Fianna Fáil's connections to FitzPatrick and Fingleton. How much did the fact of being 'well-liked' contribute, even 'unconsciously', to the fatefully bad decision to make Anglo and Nationwide's debts the responsibility of the Irish people? Honohan manages to imply that it was indeed a factor but flees from this conclusion like a man who has opened the wrong door and seen a mangled corpse. This is not a matter to be discussed in polite company.

Less culpably, but no less tellingly, the National Economic and Social Council pointed out soon after the crash that Ireland did not have a crisis, it faced five crises. It listed these as a banking crisis, a crisis in the public finances, an economic crisis, a social crisis caused by mass unemployment, and a reputational crisis after the revelation of so much bad behaviour. This was a very useful summary, and NESC rightly criticised the focus on two of these crises – banking and the public finances – at the expense of the other three. What NESC did not say, however, was that there is a sixth crisis, one that encompasses all of the others: the political crisis.

This political problem is not just about Fianna Fáil or even about the larger culture it embodies. It is about the very existence of a functioning political community. The official reaction to the banking crisis is in fact predicated on the absence of just such a community. It assumes that the most momentous political decision in the history of the state can be taken and carried through with little public support, no real parliamentary oversight and no sustained public reaction. It is predicated, in other words, on passivity.

And yet the passivity that is seen as an asset in executing the banking strategy is understood to be a barrier to any kind of long-term economic recovery. All the strategies for future economic prosperity are based on the 'smart economy', on creativity and innovation, on the ability of people to engage with new ideas, create new products and embrace new technologies. Even at the simplest level, none of this adds up – dumb politics don't create smart economies. Disengaged fatalistic zombies – which is what most citizens are meant to be in the political sphere – don't dance into a brighter economic future.

This book addresses the political crisis, not all the other aspects of the catastrophe. It is not my contention that political transformation will in itself solve Ireland's deep economic and fiscal problems. But I do contend that without political transformation there can be no solutions to the economic and fiscal crises. To get itself out of the hole it's in, Ireland will have to become an extremely well-run and deeply engaged society. It will have to have a set of common goals that can animate a sense of collective purpose. It will need a map – even if it does not exactly match the contours of a rough terrain – that gives it the courage to find its way home. None of these things is remotely on offer in the current political system. None is likely to be created by a mere change of government, from one led by a clapped-out populist right-of-centre party to one led by a fresher, hungrier right-of-centre populist party.

Most current political debate in the Western world is organised around a clash between the left's argument for a strong state and the right's argument for a strongly engaged society. In the depths of its despair, Ireland badly needs both. And I believe that these ideas can be fused in what is a rather old concept – that of the republic. A republic can and should be a state that draws its strength from the active and independent engagement of its citizens.

I set out in what follows what I believe to be an entirely realistic set of principles on which a new republic can be built. Some may find these suggestions too modest and insufficiently ambitious. But I believe that there is a natural time frame for a programme of change – the short period between now and the hundredth anniversary of the 1916 Rising in which a republic was declared but from which it never flowed. There is nothing here that cannot be done by 2016. There could be no better way of honouring the ideal of that failed republic than the achievement of a republic worth living for – and in.

PART ONE

Five Myths

The portly comedian Jo Brand has a joke that goes 'I'm an anorexic. I must be anorexic because when I look in the mirror, I see a fat person.' Brand's quip captures a larger truth – you can look at yourself in the mirror. You can see an accurate reflection. But you can still draw the wrong conclusions.

Ireland since the crash is a bit like that. It is looking very hard in the mirror. The face that stares back is no longer the one that told us we were the fairest of them all. It is gaunt with anxiety, furrowed with despair and red with rage. But while this new image may be more accurate than the previous one, it is not necessarily more truthful. Switching from an inflated self-image to a miserably deflated one is not quite the same thing as getting a clear sense of who and where we are. What matters is how we interpret what we see. To do that in a way that opens up real possibilities for change, we first have to clear away some potent myths.

Self-delusion is not uncommon. As individuals, as communities and as nations, we cannot bear too much reality. Life is hard and would be even harder if we did not leaven it with myths, fantasies and impossible dreams. Societies are so complicated that, in order to hold them in our heads, we have to simplify them. Uncertainties are so abundant that, in order to keep going, we have to ignore them. Injustices are so raw that, in order not to be beaten down by them, we have to give them only sporadic attention. Ireland and the Irish do not, in this regard, fundamentally differ from anyone else.

If the existence of self-delusion in Ireland in the first decade of the twenty-first century was not unusual, however, the degree of collective misapprehension was rather extreme. Many people knew, from their bitter daily experiences of poverty, abandonment and squalor, that everything was not for the best in the best of all possible worlds. Some people said so, repeatedly. But such experiences and such voices were powerless against an overwhelming consensus that the bad days of Irish history were over and would never come back. The idea that Ireland had found salvation in its embrace of so-called free-market globalisation ceased to be an ideology and acquired the irrefutable authority of 'common sense'. However many warnings were given, however many reasons for deep unease, the shattering of the dream in September 2008 came as a genuine shock. It was as unexpected and as appalling as a natural disaster. So profound was the self-delusion, indeed, that most of the Irish political, administrative and media elite continued to believe that what had happened was an unfortunate, albeit grim, setback on the road to nirvana and that all that was needed in response were, in a phrase much used by the Taoiseach Brian Cowen, 'temporary adjustments'.

A consensus as powerful as this has to be based on assumptions nobody really thinks about because they are simply taken for granted. But if we start to examine those assumptions, they crumble. A new realism has to begin with the reality that the economic disaster has deep roots in Irish political and institutional culture. Nothing will change unless politics are reinvented. That reinvention begins with the realisation that five underlying 'truths' of Irish politics are not true at all.

I

The Myth of the Republic

The name 'the Republic of Ireland' trips off the tongue. No such place exists.

When he was asked during the Spanish Civil War to contribute to a set of statements by writers on the conflict, Samuel Beckett's reply was typically laconic. Beckett's response came on a card on which was printed simply UPTHEREPUBLIC! As a declaration of support for the Spanish republic in its fight against the military uprising led by General Franco, this could hardly be more straightforward and unambiguous. But at a more private level, the message also carried something else that was typical of Beckett, a sardonic irony. For one of the great Irishmen of the twentieth century, it was easier to declare support for a Spanish republic than for an Irish republic. By taking possession of an Irish slogan that had been used by both Sinn Fein and Fianna Fáil, and that had little appeal for him, Beckett was making a joke on both himself and Ireland. He knew very well that in Ireland being a republican meant something quite different from what it meant in a broader European context. Beckett thus summarised in thirteen letters the strange situation of a country in which people who regarded themselves as republican might be at odds with the political realities of the republic itself.

The notion of republican democracy has deep roots in Irish

political history and, after the 1916 Rising and its proclamation of an Irish republic, it became the emotional framework within which the Irish state emerged. The Irish Republic existed both as a goal that would be realised some day, when Ireland was united, and as a theoretical reality in the state that took shape between the early 1920s and the late 1940s. On the level of rhetoric, appeals to 'the Republic established in 1916' have always had a heady potency.

It is instructive, however, to consider what the putative founders of the Republic thought it should be. The first Dáil of January 1919 – the most representative parliament that had yet sat in Ireland – was the institutional heir to the would-be revolutionaries of 1916. It adopted the Democratic Programme, which is striking for the way it defines a republic not by what it *is* but by what it *does*. And what it does is overwhelmingly concerned with the treatment of the most vulnerable citizens – the young and the old.

In fewer than 600 words, the Democratic Programme sets out a number of principles, both theoretical and practical. It affirms that 'all right to private property must be subordinated to the public right and welfare'. It sets down the governing ideals as 'Liberty, Equality, and Justice for all'. It declares the right of every citizen to an 'adequate share of the produce of the Nation's labour'. Turning to the practical values of public policy, it boldly affirms that 'It shall be the first duty of the Government of the Republic to make provision for the physical, mental and spiritual well-being of the children, to secure that no child shall suffer hunger or cold from lack of food, clothing, or shelter'. And if the welfare of children is to come first, the second and third priorities will be care for the elderly and the creation of a decent health system:

The Irish Republic fully realises the necessity of abolishing the present odious, degrading and foreign Poor Law
System, substituting therefor a sympathetic native scheme
for the care of the Nation's aged and infirm, who shall
not be regarded as a burden, but rather entitled to the
Nation's gratitude and consideration. Likewise it shall
be the duty of the Republic to take such measures as will
safeguard the health of the people and ensure the physical
as well as the moral well-being of the Nation.[1]

It is not accidental that the Democratic Programme was
barely referred to again. (Politicians much preferred the vagu-
er, more grandiose rhetoric of the 1916 proclamation.) After
Independence, the Programme's delineation of the defining
characteristics of the Republic was a hideous embarrassment.
In the real Ireland, private property almost always trumped
the common good. Neither liberty, equality or justice for all
was obvious in a society that imposed severe restrictions on
private and intimate behaviour, that tolerated vicious poverty and that excluded and exported a huge proportion of
its population. The Programme's belief that the welfare of
children would be the first concern of Irish governments was
grotesquely mocked in the hellish industrial school system in
which 170,000 children (more than one child in every hundred) were incarcerated.[2] Even the 'odious, degrading and
foreign' workhouses were left in place, albeit with the friend-
lier, more Irish name of 'county homes'. If what the framers
of the Democratic Programme outlined is called a Republic,
some other word entirely has to be invented for the state that
actually emerged from their struggles.

Perhaps, in hindsight, it was never likely that a real republic
would be born in the circumstance of early twentieth-century

Ireland. Mainstream Irish nationalism paid little attention to Ulster Protestant identity (which it simply dismissed, in the words of the 1916 Proclamation, as 'differences fostered by an alien government' to which the Republic would be 'oblivious'). That, in turn, made partition virtually inevitable. James Connolly's prediction that partition would result in a 'carnival of reaction, north and south' proved to be all too accurate, with each of the post-partition entities defining itself through its majority religious and ethnic identity.

Equally, though, the South itself may have lacked the kind of civic culture from which a republic could grow. George Russell (AE), one of the guiding spirits behind the Co-Operative Movement, argued rather presciently in 1912 that a successful democratic state could be built only on the basis of a thriving culture of citizenship: 'I understand and sympathise with the fixed passion of the politician for his theory of an Irish State, but I do not believe he will gain the results he hopes for unless his State is composed of people who may truly be called citizens.' Russell suggested that 'If we have in the country parishes of Ireland a host of unorganised peasant proprietors, each pushing a trivial agricultural business, each acting alone and never in union with his neighbours, the energy of self-interest in its lower forms will become the predominant energy, and this will overflow into rural and county councils, and we shall have frequent jobbery; and in the region of national politics we shall have the conflict of personalities, rather than the pursuit of public interests.'[3] In spite of the valiant efforts of organisations like the Co-Operative Movement itself, Russell's fears proved to be all too well-grounded. A society of peasant proprietors did not prove to be fertile ground for the growth of a republic.

Nevertheless, for well over half a century now, it has been

normal for most people living in the twenty-six counties to say that they come from 'the Republic'. It is telling, though, that even the use of this word to describe the state is mired in confusion and ambivalence. The constitution declares the name of the state to be Ireland or Eire. There is no mention of a republic. The Republic of Ireland Act of 1948 declares that 'the description of the state shall be the Republic of Ireland', but the constitution has never been amended along these lines. In bringing forward the Republic of Ireland Bill in 1948, the then Taoiseach John A. Costello explained that there would be a difference between what the state was called and what it was: 'There is the name of the State and there is the description of the State. The name of the State is Ireland and the description of the State is the Republic of Ireland.'[4]

But even as a description, the Republic barely exists. The official government website nowhere refers to the Republic of Ireland or even states that Ireland is a republic. In the diplomatic sphere, while the Irish state has accepted credentials from ambassadors addressed to 'Ireland', the 'Republic of Ireland', or the name of the president, it will not accept credentials addressed to the 'Irish Republic' because this last term was the name used in the declaration of independence in 1919 and encompassed all thirty-two counties.

All of this has little effect on the view most of the state's citizens take of their country, but the confusion is, in its own way, rather apt. If we're not sure whether to call our state a republic or not, it's partly because it is and it isn't. In the sense in which most people use the word – a liberal democracy without a monarch – Ireland obviously is a republic. But a broader notion of republicanism raises basic questions about the reality of Ireland's democracy. Using the definition articulated so powerfully in the work of Philip Pettit,[5] we can ask whether Ireland is 'a state that can operate effectively against private domination, helping to reduce the degree of domination people suffer at the hands of other individuals and groups . . . a state that is organised in such a way that it will not itself represent a source of domination in people's lives . . . a state that is conducted for the public interest, that pursues its policies in the public eye, and that acts under public control – a state that is truly a *res publica*, a matter of public business'.

The short answer to those questions is 'not really'. Far from operating against 'private domination', the Irish state has itself been run – with disastrous consequences – on behalf of private groups: bishops, professions, banks, developers. It has often been a source of domination in people's lives, especially when it operated to enforce the official morality of the Catholic church and incarcerated children and women in industrial schools and Magdalen homes. It has not been conducted in the public interest – tolerance for political and business corruption has permitted the state to be hijacked for private gain. It has not operated in the public eye – transparency and accountability have been obvious mostly by their absence. And it is not under public control – decisions of immense import, such as the bailout of the banking system, have been pushed through with very little public support.

The creation of a republic in Pettit's deeper sense isn't a matter of reading a declaration outside the General Post Office or even of enacting a constitution. It is a process that unfolds over time and that has to be renewed constantly, creatively, and with passion. In the Irish case, that process has been hampered by a number of powerful forces. All of them are reasonably obvious but because they come from different directions, their cumulative effect has been hard to define.

What they have in common is the way they have imposed limits on the emergence of a republican democracy in which public business is conducted openly, fairly, and in the public interest.

One set of limits was imposed by the overwhelmingly Catholic nature of the State established after partition. The Catholic Church didn't just enjoy the spiritual allegiance of a large majority of the population. It was also a major temporal power, with direct control over large elements of what would be regarded as the public realm in other democracies. The health and education systems were church-dominated. Specifically Catholic teaching was embodied in law in a number of areas, mostly those that related to sexuality, reproduction and marriage. So, while the state was far from the simple theocracy of caricature, it was unquestionably subject to a huge degree of direct and indirect Church influence. Practically all politicians accepted this influence as right and proper. In presenting his new constitution in 1937, Eamon de Valera proclaimed bluntly that it would present Ireland to the world 'as a Catholic nation'.

This attitude was echoed and even enhanced by the other political parties. When it took office in 1948, the Inter-Party coalition government immediately sent a message of homage to Pope Pius XII expressing its 'desire to repose at the feet of Your Holiness the assurance of our filial loyalty and our devotion to your August Person, as well as our firm resolve to be guided in all our work by the teachings of Christ and to strive for the attainment of a social order in Ireland based on Christian principles'.[6]

The effects of this subordination of state policy to Church teaching on the individual freedoms that citizens might expect in a republic were obvious. It is also worth noting, however, that these notions of 'filial loyalty', in which the Church was the stern but loving father and the state the faithful and obedient son, gave free rein to an aristocratic imagery that was, on the face of it, at odds with republican notions of civic and political equality. Having shrugged off one culture of deference to titled nobles, the new state embraced another. The elected representatives of the people always kneeled before a bishop and kissed his ring. The fact that the bishop was addressed as 'My Lord' and lived in a house that was always called a 'palace' did not seem to cause any great discomfort to Irish people who would have been enraged by any suggestion that Ireland should honour an aristocracy.

Indeed, Mary Kenny has argued persuasively that the Church occupied the place where the monarchy had been: 'even the ardent Republicans would find a vehicle for the pomp and ceremony that every society either derives from tradition or reinvents – the Holy Roman Catholic Church would soon fill the vacuum left by the departed pageantry of His Majesty.'[7] She points out that the Eucharistic Congress of 1932, which was the Irish state's first great public ceremonial, 'followed in almost every detail the format used for royal visits and royal events in Ireland . . . Not coincidentally, words and phrases previously applied to the monarchy were attached to the papacy: "allegiance", "loyalty", and "kingship" (of Christ).' The 'parallel monarchy' of the Church preserved all the habits of awe, obedience and humility that might have been thrown off in a genuinely democratic revolution.

That deference is well and truly gone, and the political power of the Church collapsed with remarkable rapidity in the 1990s. But it has left behind a problematic legacy of Church control in crucial areas of education and health. The real problem with Church dominance of public services in a democracy is that the Church itself is, explicitly and emphatically, not a democracy. It is a hierarchical organisation in which decisions come from the top down. Ideas of openness, transparency and accountability are largely irrelevant to the way it operates. And while that may not be a problem for citizens in their spiritual lives, it becomes a very severe problem indeed when key parts of the state, especially in its health and education systems, are effectively controlled by the Church.

The most extreme manifestation of this problem in recent years has been the way Church authorities dealt with revelations of child abuse by priests, brothers and nuns by seeing these basic issues of human rights and legality as essentially internal matters governed by canon law and the short-term interests of the institution. But there is also a less dramatic, if no less corrosive, conflict between, on the one hand, republican notions of the equal entitlement of citizens to public goods, and, on the other, the persistence of private church power in the provision of those goods. It is by no means an irresolvable conflict but it is one that needs to be recognised in an increasingly diverse and pluralist society.

The second obvious set of limitations on the emergence of a republic in Ireland has been the way the very notion of republicanism, which ought to act as a bulwark against private domination, has instead been an instrument of private domination. The language of Irish political discourse, in which a 'republican' meant someone associated with or supportive of the IRA, expresses this paradox. The existence throughout the history of the state of a secret and self-appointed cabal, accountable to no one but itself yet claiming to act on behalf of the Irish Republic, has tended to discredit the idea of republicanism. It has brought a mixture of tragedy and farce to any discussion of the subject. When a secret body claims to be 'the Government of Ireland', as the IRA Army Council always did, the whole notion of popular sovereignty is thrown into comic absurdity. When it then goes on to claim the right to use extreme violence on behalf of the people, that notion is fouled with blood and madness.

Less directly, the ideology of this kind of republicanism has had a broader effect on political life in the twenty-six counties. It interacted with mainstream political nationalism to create the feeling that the Irish state was a temporary arrangement, at best a mere way-station on the road to the true Republic of a United Ireland that would emerge at some time in the future. In the 1980s the former Taoiseach Charles Haughey remarked that 'When I talk about my Ireland I am talking about something that is not yet a complete reality. It is a dream that has not yet been fulfilled.' This feeling that the state was unreal, dream-like and incomplete was rooted in the political rhetoric that defined the republic as the entity declared in 1916 but never actually created. The ambivalence of much of the political class about the state it governed added to the feeling that a real republic was, in a sense, an impossible concept, relegated to the realm of aspirations, and therefore beyond the reach of practical politics.

The third longstanding limitation on the process of creating an Irish republic is corruption. If, in Pettit's phrase, a republic is a 'state that is conducted for the public interest', then corruption is the antithesis of republicanism. Political corruption is the subordination of the public interest to private interest. Its purpose is mirrored in its means of operation: it is carried out beyond public scrutiny, as a set of private understandings. But it also requires a corrosion of the idea of the public interest itself. Political decisions that

are made for private reasons – to favour those who have fa-
voured the politician – have to be justified by reference to an
invented set of public policies. This is a wider process, and
one that has in some cases drawn the institutions of the state
– including the Oireachtas, the justice system, the Revenue
Commissioners and the civil service – into unknowing collusion with corruption.

The natural corollary of corruption is cynicism. Republics
run on trust – a fuel that dried up a long time ago in Ireland.
It is generally held that the disillusionment with democracy
that became evident in the low turnouts in elections in the
1990s was caused by the revelations of the various tribunals
of inquiry in political scandals. But it is worth remembering
that long before the Irish political landscape was dominated
by tribunals of inquiry, Irish people understood quite well
that they lived in a democracy where influence and power
could be bought. The idea of 'pull', where jobs, grants and
state services were assumed to be subject to the rule that 'It's
not what you know but who you know', was pervasive in
Irish life. Most people probably saw the doings of their political masters as simply a larger version of this general rule.

It's also worth looking back on an MRBI poll conducted
for an RTE *Today Tonight* programme in November 1991.
To the proposition that 'there is a Golden Circle of people in
Ireland who are using power to make money for themselves',
a massive 89 per cent agreed. Eighty-one per cent agreed
that the people in this Golden Circle were made up in equal
measure of business people and politicians. Seventy-six per
cent thought the scandals that were then beginning to emerge
'part and parcel' of the Irish economic system rather than
one-off events. Eighty-three per cent thought that the then
current scandals were merely 'the tip of the iceberg', while

84 per cent said business people involved in corrupt dealings and fraud got off more lightly than other criminals.

These assumptions pre-date the tribunals and they remind us of how little Irish people actually believed themselves to be living in a republic where the public interest was protected and all citizens interacted with the state as equals. Corruption, in this sense, was not a cloak-and-dagger affair, but a vivid pattern in the fabric of public life. Much of the political and business elite involved in the Ansbacher tax evasion scheme were shaping the world that Irish people live in, not just metaphorically but literally. Meanwhile, the abuse of non-resident accounts for tax evasion was an open secret throughout the banking industry in the 1980s and 1990s.

The mixture of political corruption and conservative ideology that created and sustained this culture of tax evasion had huge long-term effects. It encouraged large sections of the Irish business class to salt away its disposable capital in unproductive offshore or bogus non-resident accounts rather than to invest it productively. It contributed to a fiscal crisis in which there was no option but to slash state spending on social programmes. This in turn meant that those who needed help were left to fend for themselves while those who had money were able to improve their relative position in society. While ordinary working people were paying tax at up to 60 per cent, many people with considerable resources were able to avail themselves of amnesties at a rate of 15 per cent or to evade tax altogether. When the boom came, the rich were in an even better position to benefit from it.

What became ever more apparent as the years went on and the revelations from the tribunals continued to unfold was that the ideal of the republic hadn't just slipped away in a process of economic and social change or been stolen from us by perfidious Albion. It had been deliberately and cynically betrayed from within. Some people at the very top of the heap had owed more loyalty to the Cayman Islands than to Ireland. Some citizens blessed with resources had turned themselves into 'bogus non-residents', here but not here, part of Ireland when the goodies were being given out but mysteriously vanishing into a virtual exile when the obligations of citizenship were to be met.

The last set of limits to the emergence of a republic was the growth of the notion that the state apparatus is an entity in itself, with interests of its own that are not necessarily the same as the public interest. This is not the kind of thing that gets stated explicitly, but it has hovered around some of the political controversies of the last twenty years. It popped up in the Tribunal of Inquiry into the Beef Processing Industry in 1991 when the then Attorney General stated that his role at the inquiry was to represent not the public interest but the state. It arose in the traumatic controversy over the infection of hundreds of women with hepatitis C by a state agency, the Blood Transfusion Service Board, when the state ended up fighting a dying woman, Brigid McCole, in court as if the state and a wronged citizen were somehow natural enemies. It ran through a series of court cases in the 1990s in which the parents of disabled children tried to get an appropriate education for their children. In those cases, the state sought to establish once and for all that citizens have only such rights as the state is willing to grant them. This notion is based on the profound belief that the state is an entity up there, above and beyond the people, with a life and a will all of its own.

The last twenty years or so has been a period in which some of these underlying limitations on the emergence of an Irish republic have been rolled back, while other problems have emerged. On the positive side of the equation, the shrinking of the political power of the Church to the kind of scale it ought to have in a democratic republic has opened up the possibility of a pluralist culture in which the idea of shared civic values is at least up for discussion. The Northern Ireland peace process and the gradual dismantling of para-militarism has created the opportunity for republicanism to be taken back from the gunmen. The tribunals and inquiries, problematic and ultimately ineffective as they were, at least shone a retrospective light onto the nature of the relation-ship between business and politics. The growing influence of European legislation has, in many cases, had a healthy effect on governance, making, for example, tendering for public projects more open. Inward migration has created a more culturally diverse society, one in which common civic values are more obviously necessary.

All of these processes are radically incomplete, however. The groundswell of change that gathered in the early 1990s either stalled or receded during the hysterical boom years. What could be so wrong with a state that was so spectacu-larly producing the goods – and not just any goods either but the glitziest of designer bling? In spite of large-scale inward migration and the growth of cultural and religious diversity, democratic control over the health and education systems was barely discussed. The peace process lost momentum and became mired in ambivalence. The revelations about cor-ruption and tax evasion lost their impact through weariness, cynicism, and the culture of impunity that ensured that few of those who were exposed suffered any great penalty.

As this cynicism took hold, the public lost its sense of out-rage and became resigned to a political culture it despised. In the early 1990s there had been a broad sense that political reform was an urgent necessity. For a time, no politician could utter a sentence that did not contain the words 'openness', 'transparency' and 'accountability', which were in such general use that they were boiled down to an acronym, OTA.

OTA gave us three pieces of legislation – the Ethics in Public Office Act, the Freedom of Information Act and the Electoral Act. Their purposes were, respectively, to set standards of behaviour for politicians; to ensure that government would be done, as the then Taoiseach Albert Reynolds put it, 'behind a pane of glass'; and to break the influence of big-money donors over political parties.

But like grunge, leggings and scrunchies, OTA was a 1990s fad. Once the economy started to lift off, there was a collective loss of interest in the idea of good government. One by one, the three pillars of OTA were allowed to crumble.

The ethics legislation turned out to be as toothless as a gummy frog. There were occasional feather-dustings for small fry. (Fianna Fáil TD Denis Foley's Ansbacher account, for example, resulted in a two-week suspension from the Dáil – in effect a paid holiday.) When it really mattered, with the revelation that the Taoiseach, Bertie Ahern, was on the take and could not produce a tax clearance certificate, the legislation was a beaten docket. The Standards in Public Office Commission made a terse announcement in September 2007, in relation to Bertie's dig-outs, that 'there is no basis on which to initiate an investigation'. That put the Ethics Act out of its misery.

The Freedom of Information Act, on the other hand, was deliberately sabotaged. Charlie McCreevy, then Minister for Finance, gutted it in 2003. 'Government papers' – the definition of which was extended – were excluded from the legislation for ten years after they were prepared. The number and type of official documents that could be excluded from the workings of the Act were extended to cover, for example, briefing materials prepared by departments for ministers who were about to answer parliamentary questions. (It would no longer be possible to discover what a minister might have said if she or he had been asked the right follow-up question.) Charges for access to information were greatly increased. The justification for these changes was summed up by the then Fianna Fáil senator Martin Mansergh as the necessity 'to balance the need for good government . . . with the right to freedom of information'.[8] The idea that transparency might not actually be inimical to good government, but essential to it, had been abandoned.

What was most significant was the complete lack of public response. Journalists and campaigning groups complained, but no one, almost literally, wanted to know. The citizenry as a whole simply gave up without a fight a right it had acquired in response to the corruption scandals of the 1990s.

And the third piece of reforming legislation, the Electoral Act, proved – for reasons that will be detailed in a later chapter – to be utterly ineffective as a means of breaking the link between money and politics. If anything, it merely added to cynicism about the nature of those links.

Most crucially of all, the limits of republicanism itself were painfully exposed during the boom years. Being a republic is not, in itself, a guarantee of social justice or even of basic decency. The theoretical equality of citizens did not prevent the classical republic of the United States of America consigning both African and native Americans to inferiority and oppression. The rhetoric of Liberty, Equality and Fraternity did not apply to France's colonial adventures or to its internal rages of anti-Semitism and racism. Republican ideals of openness and the public interest have not been the most obvious features of the life of the modern Italian republic. As the framers of the Democratic Programme in 1919 understood, a republic has to be measured by what it does rather than by what it says it is.

The great weakness of republican thinking has always been its struggle to connect a notion of political equality in which each citizen has the same weight in the determination of the public good, with the reality of economic inequality in which some citizens obviously carry more weight than others. The founding father of Irish republicanism, Theobald Wolfe Tone, wrote that 'True republicans fight only to vindicate the rights of equality and detest ever the name of a Master.' But the rich are always more equal than the poor and mastery will always be available to those who can mobilise a grossly disproportionate set of resources. Access to, or even control of, the media; the ability to exert economic pressure; the power to threaten dire consequences – all of these can determine the actions of the state at least as much as the votes of the electorate do. Republican democracy has to be given a content that goes beyond the nature of political institutions, and that content has to centre on equality. In the boom years, however, the political system – and to some extent public attitudes – were dominated by the idea that inequality was a necessary (and therefore implicitly desirable) condition for the creation of wealth.

For all these challenges, however, the republic is still an ideal that can frame the search for a public morality in a despairing Ireland. What makes it indispensable is that it addresses the great problem of, on the one hand, having a nation state that is the focus of collective identity and, on the other, the tendency of such identities to become exclusive, static and smug. For much of the last twenty years, it was possible to imagine that this problem would eventually go away because the nation state itself would disappear into regional and global institutions like the European Union. With the banking crisis, however, that illusion has been shattered. The state is back with a bang – as the entity that has to both underpin all economic activity and pick up the pieces when everything falls apart. We need nation states but, in a globalised culture, we need them to be based on much more than nationalism. We need them to be republics in Pettit's sense – able to define and underpin a common public interest and working against domination by particular interests, not themselves becoming sources of domination. Even if the idea of an Irish republic had not existed before, we would have to invent it now.

That idea still contains many of the things that people at the start of the twentieth century, about to embark on the painful process of inventing a modern nation, wanted from it: a sense of justice, a feeling of belonging, a commitment to protecting the weak and vulnerable, a capacity to be proud of ourselves, a notion, however vague, that there was an 'ourselves' to be proud of.

The precise content of that notion was hard to pin down back then, but it was later made concrete and tangible by its obvious absence. In an odd way, all of the revelations and disasters of the last two decades, by pointing up the absence of a public community of which Irish people could be proud, served to remind them that they still wanted one. The joys of shopping, however enthusiastically embraced, didn't quite fill the hole where a society called 'Ireland' should be. Retail therapy didn't quite assuage the anguish of finding ourselves, at the start of a new century, right back where we had started the old one, in an unsettled, fluid and desperately troubled place that needed to be re-invented as a republic.

It is striking that, as the scale of the economic and banking crisis became clear in the last two years, many people (including the present author) independently reached for the idea of the Second Republic. It was meant to convey the idea of a need to begin again, to build as if from scratch, a set of public and political institutions worthy of the allegiance of the Irish people. On reflection, however, the concept had one obvious flaw. How could there be a second republic when there was no first republic? The task is not to rediscover or reinvent a lost republic. It is to build something we have never had.

2

The Myth of Representation

What are politicians for? Most Irish people seem to believe
that the basic function of a politician is to 'get things done' for
their constituents. They don't get things done. They clog up
the system of government and create a parody of democracy.

In January 2007 it emerged that the Fianna Fáil TD for
County Clare, Tony Killeen (now minister for defence), had
twice written to the minister for justice asking for the early
release from prison of a notorious child rapist. Joseph Nugent had been sentenced to six years in jail for the systematic
and violent sexual abuse of two young children. Nugent had
raped one of the children, then aged eight, twenty-three times
and indecently assaulted him on twenty-four occasions.

The idea of a TD seeking to use political influence on behalf of a convicted paedophile may have seemed startling. It
was, however, less an aberration in the political system than
a logical expression of that system itself. Killeen's actions
were, in fact, very similar to those of his constituency rival,
Fine Gael's Pat Breen, who put down a parliamentary question to the minister for justice, asking when Nugent would be
eligible for early release.

In 2002, the Progressive Democrats junior minister, Bobby
Molloy had to resign when it was revealed that he had made
numerous representations on behalf of another child rapist,

Patrick Naughton, who viciously abused his daughter over a period of six years, beginning when she was nine, and who had tried to rape her when she was in hospital after making a complaint against him. Molloy's secretary had even attempted to contact the judge in Naughton's case, seeking to establish whether he had received letters from Naughton's sister claiming that there had been errors in his trial. In one of his letters to the minister for justice, Molloy asked whether Naughton, who had specifically threatened his daughter with retribution on his release, 'must remain in prison until the appeal is heard or can he be released?'

When these letters – fifteen in all – were published, the then Taoiseach Bertie Ahern insisted that they did not constitute grounds for resignation. Molloy had been wrong to have his secretary contact the judge, but writing to the minister for justice about the sentencing of a child rapist was just normal politics: 'because that's what politicians do. A Teachta Dála (TD) is a public representative and you make representations.'[1] The idea that 'that's what politicians do' in Ireland was accurate enough. After the fuss over Molloy had died down, they carried on doing so. The Cork Labour TD Kathleen Lynch wrote a letter to a judge in 2008 to tell him that a convicted rapist of two children came from 'a good family'. The Green Party junior minister Trevor Sargent wrote to gardaí on a number of occasions from 2007 onwards urging them to drop charges against a constituent accused of assault.

The Killeen case reinforced the idea that making pleas on behalf of paedophiles whose families have votes in their constituencies is part of 'what politicians do' in Ireland. But it also threw up, almost by accident, a remarkable statistic. Killeen explained his two letters on behalf of Nugent by saying that they had been written 'by his constituency office . . . in good faith, but without his consent'. He had merely intended to inquire about Nugent's state of health, not to request his early release. When asked whether he had in fact read the letters before they were sent, he said he had not. To give substance to this apparently remarkable claim, he pointed out that 'his constituency office had issued more than 220,000 letters'.[2]

Killeen had, at that stage, been a member of the Dáil for fourteen years. That's a maximum of 3,640 working days. To have sent out 220,000 letters, his office would have had to issue 60.4 representations on behalf of constituents *every working day*. Each one of these letters – presumably to government departments, state agencies and local councils – would have to be dealt with by civil and public service bureaucrats. If we make the extremely conservative assumption that each representation would in turn generate a minimum of five other pieces of internal and external correspondence (files passed up and down the bureaucratic chain of command; the drafting and re-drafting of formal replies to the TD's representation; letters back to the TD) this gives us one TD generating at least 300 actions within the bureaucracy on every working day. If Killeen is at all typical of his peers in the Dáil (and there is nothing to suggest that any of them regard him as unusual), the 166 TDs would be responsible for demanding 49,800 actions from the civil or public service every working day. Over the 260 working days in a year, that's an annual total of almost 13 million pieces of internal and external correspondence generated by TDs.

This whirling blizzard of paper-pushing is Kafkaesque; much of it is entirely meaningless. Most of this 'representation' of constituents by TDs falls into one of three categories of uselessness. It is either (a) improper, (b) misdirected or (c) unnecessary. In the first category are things TDs should not be doing at all – trying to influence the justice system in favour of child rapists is a pretty good example. In the second are things that are properly the function of local government. Anecdotally, most TDs suggest that a great deal of what they are asked to deal with by constituents, and indeed a great deal of what they are asked about on the doorsteps even during general elections, is the domain of the local council – roads, street lights, public parks, housing allocations and so on. This is why, after legislation prohibited TDs from being county or city councillors, so many ensured that a close ally or family member 'inherited' their council seat. (This applies even at the top level of national politics: both Barry Cowen, brother of Taoiseach Brian, and Henry Kenny, brother of Fine Gael leader Enda, are prominent county councillors.) In 2008, nine councillors were not merely members of a TD's family but were actually employed by the TD (at public expense) as parliamentary assistants or secretaries. One TD, Jackie Healy-Rea, explained the 'huge advantage' of having his son Michael as a member both of his own staff and of Kerry County Council: 'Glory be to God, that keeps him in closer touch more of the time with the people of the constituency, and not alone is he able to pass on the Dáil problems to me, he's also in a position to help these people with county council problems.'[3]

The third category of useless representations is that in which either TDs can do nothing or in which there are perfectly adequate independent mechanisms for dealing with problems. The statutory Citizens Information Board provides 'free, impartial and confidential information' on access to public services from 106 citizens' information centres and

162 outreach centres in every part of the country. The office
of the Ombudsman deals with complaints of maladministration by public services and government departments. There
is little evidence that TDs can actually do very much that
these agencies can't. Indeed, as long ago as the late 1960s, a
famous study of machine politics in County Donegal found
politicians' 'claims of effective intervention' on behalf of the
voter to be 'imaginary patronage' because 'the parties' real
control over the distributive institution is quite limited'. The
TD's claim to be the power broker is generally based on 'illusion and manipulation'.[4]

Yet this 'imaginary patronage' is essentially what TDs do
– being in parliament is a sideline to the main activity of pre-
tending to be delivering benefits to constituents. TDs themselves reported in a 2010 study that they spend on average
53 per cent of their time on 'constituency work', and just 38
per cent on legislative work.[5] For every hour the average TD
spends on legislative work, one hour and twenty-five minutes
is spent on constituency-related issues. And this is, moreover,
the way they see themselves. They report that they 'typically
see their role as being primarily constituency representatives.
They rate constituency-based activities as more important
than legislative activities.' Asked to list their activities in order
of priority, TDs gave the top three as: working on individual
constituents' cases; lobbying on behalf of the general interest
of your constituency; and visiting your constituency/deliver-
ing leaflets on your work. None of these activities, of course,
has anything to do with the actual work of parliament.

It is important to note that most of this 'constituency work'
is not really work for the constituency. It is not about proposing or opposing projects that would benefit or harm the community as a whole. The biggest chunk of 'constituency work'

(50 per cent) is the pursuit of personal issues for individual voters either through the activity that is universally known as 'persecuting civil servants' or by putting down parliamentary questions on their behalf. Another 25 per cent of this time is campaigning – going to funerals, handing out leaflets, turning up at events. Just 25 per cent of the time spent on 'constituency work' is actually categorised by TDs themselves as 'lobbying on behalf of one's constituency'.

The politicians wouldn't be selling these services if there were not plenty of willing buyers. In the 2002 Irish National Election Study, an astonishing one in five people reported having made contact with a TD in the preceding five years. In the 2007 study, 60 per cent of voters said they expected a TD to provide 'a local service'. This frantic clientelism appeals to two strong notions in Irish culture. One is localism. Especially in rural Ireland, there is still a sense that the state is 'them up in Dublin' – an abstract and potentially hostile entity whose potential malevolence needs to be warded off and whose potential for good needs to be exploited by cunning. The other is the concept of 'pull'. Rooted in the experiences of both the extended family (in which notions of mutual obligation to provide a leg-up were deeply engrained) and of emigration (in which having a network of pre-established contacts was often crucial for survival), its persistence into the twenty-first century owes much to the needs of the political system itself.

The more impersonal the state actually becomes – the less open it is to personal intervention – the more important it has been for politicians to keep alive an almost mystical idea of 'pull' in which the idea of having an insider working the system on your behalf gives that system the illusion of a personal intimacy it actually lacks. There is, in this culture, a perverse pleasure in securing by means of illusory 'pull' a benefit to which one is actually entitled. The thought – however mistaken – of having secured it against the grain doubles its value.

This system is, of course, the opposite of citizenship. As well as having duties, citizens have rights. They expect the public services for which they pay to be responsive to their needs and are angry when they fail them. The entire edifice of clientelism depends on the assumption that the clients do not have entitlements. While citizens are conscious of their own power, clientelism thrives on perceived powerlessness. Public services have to be bought, not with money (which, after all, the people have already provided through their taxes), but with the currency of the system – votes. Interaction with the state occurs within a kind of marketplace – the politician's mediation has an implied price: the 'number one' at the next election.

Even the language of this exchange is telling. Politicians don't meet their constituents. They 'hold clinics' or even 'surgeries'. The governing metaphor is medical. The implied relationship of power is that of doctor/TD to patient/constituent. Even the physical procedure is similar: the queue in the waiting area before being ushered into the presence of the expert behind the desk, the quietly confidential and soothing discussion of the symptoms and the reassuring piece of paper as an end product – the prescription in one case, the letter to the government department in the other. In both cases, of course, the prescription may be a placebo. (It may be no coincidence that a disproportionate number of TDs are GPs – for both the politician and the voter, the transition comes quite naturally.) The implication is not simply that the doctor knows best and that the patient is in a subordinate and essentially passive role. It is also that it is the constituent with the problem who is sick. The system itself is of course perfectly healthy.

Radical political reform in Ireland has to involve the destruction of this culture. To have any realistic prospect of success, however, that process of reform has to start, not with the Dáil itself, but with local government. There are three closely interrelated reasons for this.

The first is that we can be sure of one thing – change sure as hell isn't going to start from the top. Irish political, administrative, professional, media and business elites are far too deeply entrenched to have any interest in radical reform. The systems of governance may have experienced a catastrophic failure, but they have no intention of being accountable for it. And they have shown themselves to be remarkably tenacious in the face of their own abject failure. Their talent for survival far outweighs their admittedly limited talents in all other areas.

The second reason for starting with the local is that without real local government what will continue to happen is what has always happened in Ireland – we get local politicians operating at national level, and indeed national politicians continuing to function as if they were country councillors. (To take one outstanding example, Willie O'Dea, one of the poster boys of clientelism and a long-standing member of the cabinet, employed six civil servants from his department to look after his constituency work and sent constituency correspondence on departmental notepaper.)

The third reason for starting with local government is precisely because localism remains so strong. Irish people have a very weak sense of ownership of the state, but a very strong sense of local belonging. John McGahern wrote of his home county of Leitrim:

> It is each single enclosed locality that matters and everything that happens within it is of passionate interest to those who live there. 'Do you have any news – any news?' But once that news crosses a certain boundary, eyes that a moment before were wild with curiosity will suddenly glaze. News no longer local is of no interest.[6]

McGahern was writing of a rural Ireland that has greatly changed, but that broad sense of the nature of passionate engagement remains valid. Even during the apparently deep disruptions of the boom years, when new communities were suddenly established in the commuter belts of the major cities, there was a remarkable ability to create, almost from scratch, a strong sense of local identity.

Nor is this dominance of the local entirely deplorable. If, on the one hand, it has disabled national politics, it has also, on the other, supported the extraordinary vigour of voluntary and community organisations. Ireland has some of the best civil society organisations in the world, all of them built on a very strong sense of local engagement and participation. From the Gaelic Athletic Association, which is probably the most successful amateur sporting organisation in the world, to leading development agencies like Concern and Trocaire, there is a culture of achievement and excellence that is so often lacking in the official realm.

The mystery, indeed, is why this vigorous civil society has translated into such a static and decrepit political culture. The answer, surely, lies in the extreme poverty of local government. Rather than building on and seeking to give an institutional shape to passionate localism, the political system has done its best to ensure that those energies remain politically inert.

The Irish state is one of the most centralised in the developed world: 94 per cent of decisions on public expenditure are made at national level. In Ireland, local government accounts for only 12.7 per cent of public employment. In Britain, the corresponding figure is 52.3 per cent. In Denmark – the EU country to which Ireland is most comparable in terms of scale and history – it is 70.8 per cent. The range of functions allocated to Irish local authorities is the narrowest in Europe. Half of local government funding comes from the state, making it essentially impossible for councils to have any meaningful financial independence. Whereas in developed democracies, local authorities have large powers in areas like taxation, education, health, policing and economic development, in Ireland they have virtually none.[7]

Perhaps because it was so fragile when it was established in the midst of civil war or perhaps, less grandly, because its early political elites wanted to concentrate power and patronage in their own hands, local government was systematically weakened throughout the early decades of the state. Emboldened by justified public cynicism about the levels of corruption and 'jobbery' in local councils, the Free State government abolished boards of guardians and rural district councils and resurrected old Westminster powers to dissolve uncooperative local authorities. (A total of twenty elected bodies were replaced by appointed commissioners in the first three years of the State.)[8] Fianna Fáil, when it took power in 1932, adopted the same approach. A government memorandum of 1933 noted that 'With the establishment of a central administration responsible to the people as a whole, and with modern improvements in transport and communications, governmental intervention and supervision is now feasible in respect of all national activities. The retention of local government is, therefore, gradually becoming an expensive anachronism.'

This proved to be a self-fulfilling prophecy. As local power shifted ever further towards city and county managers appointed by central government – the management system was formalised in 1942 – councils became increasingly meaningless. In 1978, local authorities lost much of their remaining independence when Fianna Fáil abolished local property taxes (domestic rates). In areas in which elected councillors retained powers – particularly planning and zoning – they often tended to use that power irresponsibly and in some cases corruptly, further weakening the argument for shifting power back to elected representatives and away from managers and central government.

But the exercise of central control hardly proved to be a model of corruption-free strategic planning either. Government departments ended up as fussy micromanagers. It is worth stressing that this whole process has been disastrous for central as well for local government. Instead of being centres for strategic thinking, innovation, coordination and long-term planning, government departments got bogged down in day-to-day bureaucracy and crisis management.

As Tom Barrington noted in 1990, 'Intensive centralisation since the 1920s has been a ghastly failure, with central government sinking into a sludge of detailed business that clogs channels of decision, swamps strategic issues, frustrates initiatives and bureaucratises the whole.'

Indeed one of the side effects of the absence of real local government has been the growth of the quangocracy. Since the state bureaucracy could not in fact cope with all the demands of both local and national government, it ended up outsourcing much of the business of government to unelected and largely unaccountable 'public bodies'. In 1927 Ireland had four such bodies. In 1990 there were a hundred and in 1998, 130. In 2006 Paula Clancy and Grainne Murphy identified no fewer than 450 such bodies at a national level. These bodies created a vast network of governmental patronage, with 5,000 appointments to boards in the gift of the government of the day, almost entirely without parliamentary scrutiny or oversight.[9] And this process has been mirrored in local administration, where twenty-two types of agencies, totalling 491 different bodies, are in operation. The result is that decisions that affect people's lives have been moved further and further beyond their control and, in many cases, even beyond their knowledge.

The most spectacular example of this process is, of course, the establishment of the Health Service Executive in 2005. The HSE replaced the eleven regional health boards, which were strongly linked to local councils. It was generally agreed that there were too many health boards and too much overlap in their bureaucracies. But they did have some real mechanisms for accountability – their chief executives had to appear regularly before the boards, which included elected local politicians. In deciding to abolish the boards, the government didn't end the overlap of functions – it simply amalgamated everything in one huge bureaucracy. And it made that bureaucracy much more unaccountable than it had been before.

This shift crystallised the way the lack of local democracy atrophies national as well as local government. The abolition of all local control over health services hugely enhanced the centralised power of the minister for health. But this power is now exercised in the classic Irish way – the minister refers most questions to the HSE, which has no obligation to answer them promptly. At least half of Dáil questions on health issues are routinely referred to the HSE, which may eventually provide an answer that cannot be followed up. When scandals are revealed, the minister complains about the HSE as if it were a distant and foreign power, entirely unrelated to her functions. Thus, for example, Mary Harney's response in 2010 to the revelation of the deaths of children in HSE care: 'serious questions have to arise of course for people who have responsibility, very serious questions'. If only these people could be found, 'people would lose their jobs'. Unfortunately, the 'people who have responsibility' for identifying the 'people who have responsibility' are the HSE themselves: 'it is a matter for the board of the HSE ultimately or the CEO of the HSE to decide'.[10] The net effect, in terms of the functioning of Irish democracy, of the removal of any local control over health services was to create the bureaucratic dream of a system in which no one can ever be held responsible for anything.

The need for a radically new system of local democracy should therefore be obvious. Three factors, though, account for a reluctance to face that necessity.

The first is the idea that Ireland is too small and has too dispersed a population to have powerful local authorities as well as a national government. This is simply spurious – the most powerful local democracies are in Scandinavian countries with similarly small, and in some cases even more widely dispersed, populations.

The second is the much more well-grounded perception that Ireland already has too many full-time politicians and does not need more. There are two answers to this objection. Since we already pay local councillors even though they are relatively powerless, it would make far more sense to pay them for actually exercising real functions. And proper local government would enable a slimming-down of the national parliament and a drastic reduction in the quangocracy. Indeed, one of the attractions of starting democratic reform at a local level is that it helps to clarify the question of exactly what TDs (and, God help us, Senators) are for and how many we really need. It would also enable a clear-out of many of the unaccountable 'public bodies' whose functions would be taken over by local democracy.

The establishment of proper local governments would also involve a rationalisation in the number of local councillors. Currently, there is a complete lack of consistency in the number of electors for each councillor. There are 1,117 electors per councillor in Leitrim county council compared with 5,784 electors per councillor in Cork county council. Dublin city council has 6,717 electors per councillor while in Galway city council, the ratio is 2,955 electors to one councillor. By ending these anomalies, the overall number of councillors can be reduced.

The third and most serious objection is that it would be madness to give local politicians more powers when they have so often made a mess of the ones they have. Abysmal planning contributed shamefully to the fatal property mania of boomtime Ireland. Councils permitted the building of 550,000 housing units between January 1996 and December 2005, while the number of households grew by just 346,000. Thereafter, the council areas with the largest numbers of vacant houses were the ones that continued to build most frantically. They are also the ones that have continued, even since the collapse of the property boom, to zone more land for development. Building in flood plains, plonking suburban estates in rural landscapes or swamping existing villages with grossly disproportionate housing schemes – all of these have been standard practice in some parts of the country.

Not all of this is the fault of elected councillors alone and some councils were more responsible than others. Many local politicians have immensely honourable records of fighting for the public interest. But it would be foolish to deny that much of the carry-on at council re-zoning sessions has been disgraceful. Even when bribery has not been an issue, some of this behaviour brings to mind George Orwell's quip about how one cannot bribe a British journalist but 'seeing what the man will do unbribed, there's no occasion to'.

This is a very serious objection, but it also goes to the heart of the necessity for genuinely radical change. In the first place, if Irish people are going to elect crooks and clowns, if they have learned nothing from the catastrophe that decrepit politics has created, there is little else to be said. The rest is silence, except for the squeaking of the wheels on the handcart in which what's left of the country is going to Hell.

The other point, though, is crucial. Local government has been caught in a vicious circle. Because it has been relatively powerless, voters have not been too bothered by the poor quality of many of their councillors. Because those councillors have so often behaved like clowns, contempt for local councils has deepened and expectations have eroded.

The key to breaking through this circle is funding. Local democracy works in other countries because councillors are spending local money. Local taxes – especially on property – pay for services that are delivered in the community. People can see what they're getting – or not getting – for their money. They have every incentive to enforce accountability and to demand competence. In Ireland, because local taxation is so weak, this link is broken. People have not been able to make a clear connection between the money that is raised in their own neighbourhoods and the services they get in return. They have not been forced to articulate their own priorities and watch their money being spent on the things they say they want. Neither has it been clear to them that they literally pay a price if they elect idiots or tolerate shysters. The knowledge that local people would have to pay for the extra costs of bad planning decisions through higher local taxes would surely have a salutary effect.

At the moment, no one really counts the cost of bad planning decisions. The simple reality is that highly dispersed houses cost far more to service than properly planned villages and towns. But all the pressure on local politicians and planners in rural Ireland is to permit the construction of one-off houses, each of which requires, for example, its own one-to-one connection to the electricity network. In 2009 almost half (46 per cent) of all houses completed in Ireland fell into this category. In one council – Galway County Council – one-off houses made up 80 per cent of total completions in 2009, while for another five councils they accounted for more than 70 per cent, with Kilkenny and Mayo at 75 per cent, Leitrim at 74 per cent, Roscommon at 73 per cent and Monaghan at 71 per cent.

James Nix has estimated the additional public cost of this kind of housing between 2004 and 2009 at €1 billion – including €120 million on postal services and €720 million on school transport, plus extra costs for bin collections, road maintenance, electricity and phone connections.[11] These costs can often be traced directly to decisions made by councils in permitting (and indeed encouraging) dispersed populations. But why should those councils worry about such costs, when they are mostly borne by 'them up in Dublin'? The more dispersed the population, the more national funds a council tends to get. For example, Limerick city and County Carlow both have around 23,000 households. In 2010, Limerick got €2.4 million from central government for the maintenance of local and regional roads. County Carlow got more than twice as much – €5.6 million. Likewise, the allocation for Galway county council (€23 million) was almost exactly the same as that for the five largest cities (Dublin, Cork, Galway, Limerick and Waterford) put together.

It would never be fair to impose the full extra cost of these differences on rural counties. (Even with good planning, rural life will always be more expensive.) And local government can never be entirely locally funded. (This would leave citizens in poorer regions with worse public services than those in richer ones). But the balance can be radically shifted by creating a strong and transparent link between local taxation (through property and site value taxes) and local services. This in turn would change the balance of pressures in rural Ireland by giving local people hard financial reasons to demand decent planning and to oppose expensive and unsustainable development.

It may not be possible to entirely eliminate corruption from any planning process but it is not particularly difficult to end systemic skulduggery. A proper inquiry into the role of planning authorities in the property boom would, as the National Institute for Regional and Spatial Analysis suggests, 'investigate all aspects of the planning system and its operation, including charges of localism, cronyism and clientelism where appropriate. The inquiry should not take the form of a witch hunt or a blame game, but rather constitute a systemic review of how the planning system failed to counter and control the excesses of the boom and provide a more stable and sustainable pattern of development.'[12]

Freedom of information legislation can be strengthened at local level, giving communities greater power to scrutinise what is being done. Councillors can be legally barred from engaging in occupations that create a conflict of interest with their role as planners. At the moment, local authority staff are banned from engaging in work that might create a conflict of interest, but there is no such provision for the councillors who actually make planning decisions. Councillors can, and do, act as estate agents, auctioneers, 'planning agents', 'planning consultants' and even property developers. This has to stop. No longer should the term 'local councillor and estate agent' be set in permanent type on the print systems of every provincial newspaper.

Central government can take on its proper role and set robust and legally binding standards for planning and development. The National Spatial Strategy, which was developed but effectively ditched during the boomtime frenzy, needs to be put on a statutory footing. Unsustainable practices like building in flood plains need be made illegal. Councillors should be obliged, as they are not at present, to consider the views of their professional planning staff and, if they reject them, to articulate in writing their reasons for doing so.

But the most effective safeguard against corruption and abuse in the planning process is to remove the most obvious incentive – the vast amounts of money to be made by landowners as a result of decisions by councillors to re-zone their lands for development. We already know how to do this; we've known since 1974, when the Kenny Report was published. Judge Kenny recommended that local authorities be entitled to compulsorily purchase development land at a premium of just 25 per cent over its agricultural value. The failure – by all governments – to implement Kenny has been the strongest marker of the ultimate dominance of the interests of landowners and developers over the common good. Conversely, the implementation of the Kenny recommendations now would be the strongest possible indication that that dominance has finally ended.

A new system of local government will, of course, be entirely pointless if the new local councils are merely Mini Me versions of our current dysfunctional system of national government. The new councils have to the crucibles for radical experiments in democratic participation. Democracy in Ireland has to be rebuilt from the bottom up. This process has to start with the recognition that we're not currently very good at it and have to learn. And the only way to learn democracy is by doing it.

Local governments should have elected representatives and professional managers and all the structures that are necessary to administer the greatly enhanced budgets that will come with the extension of their powers. But the other side of that power has to be a vastly increased system, not just of accountability, but of direct involvement. The local arena is ideal for 'deliberative democracy', generally defined as 'discussion in which citizens collectively and cooperatively analyze a situation; establish criteria for evaluating public responses to it; identify multiple options based on different sets of values or value priorities held by members of the public; weigh arguments for and against each option in the light of clear criteria; and, through continuing discussion (that may or may not include voting), approach a measure of agreement that (ideally) most participants can accept as a collective "decision".'

This process does not have to be invented from scratch. There are many hundreds of functioning deliberative democracy projects working in cities, town and villages worldwide. Toolkits for different kinds of projects are widely available. But in Ireland's desperate situation, the process of engaging may be more important than the precise form the engagement takes. Given their levels of anger, disillusion and perceived powerlessness, Irish people need to know that someone is listening to them – even if, to begin with, it is only themselves.

The obvious objection to this kind of process becoming part of a renewed system of self-government is that things already take far too long to get done in Ireland and that collective deliberation will simply make for further inefficiency. In fact, one of the main causes of inefficiency for major projects in Ireland is not too much consultation but too little. Typically, large-scale public or private projects come with a veneer of consultation whose only aim is to persuade the community to accept what has already been decided by those who know better. This then results in the alienation of large parts of the community, leading to objections, protests, appeals and court cases. Not all conflict can – or should – be avoided, but many of these unproductive clashes would be made redundant by having systems of genuine democratic engagement in which people had a fair say in what happens to their communities.

Anyone who thinks that the current system of top-down, management-led local government works needs to consider the debacle of the Poolbeg incinerator project in Dublin. In 1997 Dublin City Council decided to develop an incinerator. In 2007 the council – against the wishes of elected councillors

– signed a secretive contract with the American consortium Covanta to run a giant incinerator in Dublin Bay. The process is a model of scrutiny-free bureaucracy. Responsible and engaged members of the local community have been locked out: 'We have asked the council at open days, at the Environmental Protection Agency (EPA) and Bórd Pleanála oral hearings and via Freedom of Information requests for details of the original financial model and for details of the contract costings but the council refuses to divulge any details on the basis of commercial confidentiality.' No one has been allowed to see the contract that has been signed on behalf of the public. The result is not efficiency, but deadlock and potentially huge public costs.

What's true of projects is even more obviously true of services. Public services like schools, local health clinics and community policing work better when they are most responsive to the needs of those they are supposed to serve. Instead of employing consultants and marketing experts to figure out those needs, it is much more efficient (as well as more interesting) to give people the chance to articulate them for themselves.

Most importantly, we need to train ourselves to be citizens. But we don't start out in ignorance. We actually know an awful lot about organising, reaching consensus, taking responsibility for using resources well and looking out for those who need the most help. We do it all the time in voluntary organisations, especially in our communities. We need to start thinking of Ireland as a voluntary organisation – a collective we can choose to belong to but that functions only to the degree that we get involved.

3

The Myth of Parliamentary Democracy

Irish people believe they live in a parliamentary democracy. Until they grasp the rather obvious fact that they don't, they have no hope of creating a republican system of government.

In June 2009 the Labour Party spokesman on housing, Ciaran Lynch, submitted an amendment at the committee stage to the government's Housing (Miscellaneous Provisions) Bill. It was thrilling and controversial stuff, citing a particular paragraph and proposing 'to delete "2007" and substitute "2008"'. The point of the amendment was very simple. The section of the Bill made reference to 'the Health Acts 1947 to 2007'. Lynch realised that this was a mistake by the drafters of the Bill. There was now another Health Act – passed in 2008. The section should read 'Health Acts 1947 to 2008'.

This is not the stuff of great political drama, but what happened next was a perfect illustration of the Dáil's capacity for political farce. Lynch was merely being diligent and helpful. He had spotted a technical error that might, some time down the road, have caused a problem for someone looking for social housing or led to an expensive court case. But there was an obvious problem – Lynch belonged to the Opposition. The amendment was not accepted. On the next (report) stage of the legislative process in our august parliament, the minister, Michael Finneran, introduced his own amendment: 'In page

36, line 5, to delete, "2007" and substitute "2008"'.' It was carried.

Thus the Dáil, whose submissiveness to government would be considered intolerably humiliating in an S&M parlour.

The Irish parliament is probably the weakest in the democratic world. In a careful but devastating analysis in 2001, the then Ombudsman, Kevin Murphy, repeated the truism that Ireland is a parliamentary democracy under whose constitution there is a division of powers between the legislature and the executive and the government is 'responsible to Dáil Eireann'. He then went on to say something that in other societies might be considered explosive:

This model of government is posited on notions of checks and balances and accountability. Practice in recent decades suggests that, increasingly, this model is more of a theoretical construct than a reality. This may be particularly the case in terms of the actual balance of power as between the executive and the legislature and in terms of the capacity of the legislature to supervise the executive. The notion that the Oireachtas sets policy, makes the laws and then leaves it to the executive to implement the laws does not fit with how government operates in practice. The reality . . . is that the Government, once elected, controls the Houses of the Oireachtas with a resulting diminution in the capacity of the Houses to supervise the executive. For all practical purposes, it is the Government which decides policy; which proposes legislation and ensures its passage through the Oireachtas and, subsequently, in its executive capacity, ensures that the laws are implemented.[1]

The Ombudsman's analysis attracted some comment, but not much. The idea that parliamentary democracy in Ireland is 'more of a theoretical construct than a reality' did not seem to shock anyone. Indeed, it is confirmed by the basic textbooks on Irish administration. Basil Chubb, writing in *Constitution and Constitutional Change*, as long ago as 1970, notes matter-of-factly that the separation of powers 'along the lines suggested by the literal meaning of the words of the Constitution does not obtain in Ireland. It would be absurd to think of the Government as having only "executive" functions . . . it would be misleading to envisage the Oireachtas as "making laws" in the literal sense or to the extent that American congressmen, for example, are "legislators".'

Likewise, Gerard Hogan and David Gwynn Morgan's *Administrative Law in Ireland* (1998), a standard work of reference, states that 'such is the strength of the whip system that the legislature cannot be regarded as speaking with a voice independent of the executive and, so, it is realistic to characterise the central element in the Irish governmental system as a fused executive-legislature'. Parliament and government are Siamese twins and the government twin has all the muscles.

The Dáil does not make laws – it passes them. Legislation is almost never initiated by TDs. At best, they get to debate the rights and wrongs of legislation proposed by government and perhaps to make some minor amendments. But even these privileges can be taken away whenever a government chooses to do so, usually at the end of a term, when it pushes through all its unfinished business.

In one week, in July 2009, the government used the guillotine on parliamentary debates a total of thirteen times. What a guillotine means is that government amendments to legislation which have not yet been debated are deemed to have been passed and the whole Bill is then put to a vote which the government wins.

In that particular week, the Dáil was 'debating' the Criminal Justice Amendment Bill, a highly controversial piece of legislation that fundamentally alters the right to trial by jury – a historic change in the nature of Irish criminal law. The 'debate' was derisory. Government amendment number two, for example, created a long and complex list of suspicious items whose possession can be used as evidence of a crime. The amendment is 553 words long. The entire debate on the amendment is 402 words long.

There was some evidence of public disquiet at the farcically cursory nature of these proceedings. But the government got away with it, and was emboldened to go even further in its open contempt for the Dáil. Consider a single day's work – 1 July 2010, the day after it was announced that Anglo Irish Bank is officially the biggest bank failure in the world. In this one day, the Dáil 'debated' and 'scrutinised' the ratification of the Stockholm Convention on Persistent Organic Pollutants; the report and final stages of the Central Bank Reform Bill; the report and final stages of the Planning and Development Bill; and the report and final stages of the Civil Partnership Bill.

This is, by any standards, an impressive range of work. The Stockholm Convention is a very important international environmental treaty. The Central Bank and Planning bills were the key government responses to the anarchy in banking and development that had destroyed the economy. The Civil Partnership Bill was a historic step towards full equality for gay and lesbian citizens. What kind of parliament could possibly deal with all of this momentous matter in a day? Answer: one made of rubber with a large wooden handle coming out its back and the word 'Passed' carved backwards on its chest.

All of these crucial issues were debated in the way a juggernaut debates roadkill and scrutinised with the intensity that a dead man fixes on the inside of his coffin lid. The Stockholm Convention was nodded through with no discussion, explanation or examination at all. As far as the Dáil was concerned, the government might have signed up to a permanent ban on traditional music or funny hats. The Planning Bill, which had first come to the Dáil in forty sections totalling forty pages, returned for its final stage with 128 government amendments, laid out over 100 pages. (There was not even an explanatory memorandum to enable deputies to make sense of the amendments.) The time allocated for this 100 pages of amendments to be 'debated' was three and a half hours.

As for the Central Bank Bill, generally agreed to be the most important piece of legislation to be put before the Dáil in that entire term, there were fifty-six complex amendments to be debated. The debate began shortly before noon. It ended at one o'clock. No minister, senior or junior, from the Department of Finance was present (the government's position was put by the Minister for Defence – appropriately enough since his sole job was to repel parliamentary scrutiny and shoot down any stray balloons of Dáil self-esteem). In the course of an hour, the legislation was hammered through. Just thirteen of the fifty-six amendments were even formally put to the Dáil: the rest were deemed, under the guillotine system, to have been passed without any debate. Even this overstates the degree of scrutiny: seven different amendments, dealing with the important issue of the role of credit unions and how they should be regulated, were taken together. Every single speaker spoke against the government's line on this issue. Not a single government backbencher spoke at all. While the minister was replying, the *leas ceann comhairle* (deputy speaker) interrupted him to say that it was one o'clock, time for lunch, and to put the motion 'that the amendments set down by the Minister for Finance and not disposed of, are hereby made to the Bill; Fourth Stage is hereby completed; and the Bill is hereby passed'. Sixty-nine government backbenchers trooped in from their offices and voted 'yes', and the legislation was passed. Barely any of them can have had the faintest idea whether the legislation they'd voted for makes any sense at all.

But they voted for it anyway, because that's what they do. The power of a parliament is utterly dependent on the willingness of a significant number of government-aligned members to disobey their own party on certain occasions – or at least to generate a fear that they might. TDs, on the other hand, do what they're told. When asked in an Oireachtas study how they felt a TD should vote when party policy clashes with the opinion of the party's supporters in the constituency, 86 per cent of TDs answered that the TD should vote with the party. Similarly, when asked how a TD should vote when that TD disagrees with party policy, 83 per cent indicated that the TD should vote with the party. It is worth noting that the same TDs who slavishly 'serve' their constituents by flooding the bureaucratic system with representations on their behalf, do not actually believe that they should represent the views of those same constituents. There is of course a close relationship rather than a contradiction between these two notions of representation – the first is a substitute for the second. As the Oireachtas study put it, 'TDs may make a distinction between their representative role on behalf of their constituency and their voting behaviour in the Dáil.'

The myth is that TDs are elected to represent their con-

stituents in the Dáil. The reality is admitted by the TDs themselves – that they do no such thing. In the Oireachtas survey,
just twenty of seventy-three TDs said they believed that TDs
represent the views of their constituents 'very well'.

There may, meanwhile, be those who labour under the
misapprehension that TDs can at least get answers to parliamentary questions (PQs) put to ministers. Such a belief could
not long survive any contact with the system. There has indeed been a huge increase in the number of PQs – from about
5,000 a year in 1968 to almost 30,000 a year now. Most of
these, however, are written questions that have nothing to do
with the functions of national government. 'The vast majority of these written questions', says a textbook written by
two senior civil servants, 'relate to constituents' problems,
such as when payments are expected to be made under social
welfare and grant schemes of various kinds.'[2] These queries
generally achieve nothing:

> PQs have little effect on the work of civil servants beyond
> the amount of time taken up in the administrative proce-
> dure which the careful preparation of replies and notes
> entails . . . The officials preparing the replies to PQs are
> obliged . . . to drop all other work and attend to the PQs
> . . . civil servants are aware that the main reasons for
> questions on constituency matters are, firstly, to allow pol-
> iticians to represent themselves openly as advocates of the
> defenceless citizen against the powerful minister and the
> soulless bureaucrat, and, secondly, to provide them with
> written material which they can send to their constituents
> and to their local newspapers as evidence that they are
> about their constituents' business. The value of the PQ as
> a means of resolving grievances, however, is questionable.

For the most part, therefore, the purpose of all this activity is simply to generate a piece of paper which the TD can send to the constituent in order to show that something is being done: usually what was being done anyway.

As for the oral questions, usually asked of ministers by frontbench Opposition spokesmen, they are in effect answered by anonymous civil servants whose primary purpose is to hoard information like precious treasure and, in policy terms, to commit the department to as little as possible. One former civil servant, Eamon Delaney, has written that in 'answering' PQs, 'the idea was to say as little as possible . . . We had to protect the State from overly inquisitive TDs and there was no point in being garrulous and volunteering information.'[3]

What actually happens when a minister has to answer an oral question is that the civil servants prepare, on the one hand, a great deal of information in a secret file and, on the other, a bland and ambiguous reply. The minister's job is to ensure that most of the contents of the file remain where they belong – within the safe keeping of the department. The point of all the time and effort (paid for, of course, by the hapless citizen) expended in this process is to produce information and then *not* release it. In this respect, the Dáil is like a bar run by the Pioneer Total Abstinence Association.

One study sums up the process: 'Preparing replies to PQs takes up a lot of time within government departments, but the final responses to questions as delivered by ministers will give very little of the detail supplied by the department. Furthermore, when drafting replies to PQs, civil servants naturally tend to argue their case rather than admit errors or seek compromise. In the Dáil, debates or statements on the minister's reply are not permitted. Also, the Ceann Comhairle has no power to ensure the questioner receives a satisfactory response. Interviews by this author suggest that answers to PQs have deteriorated in recent years as ministers wished to avoid future accusations on a particular issue.'[4]

Pretty much everyone knows, therefore, that there is no separation of powers, that there are no checks and balances, no real accountability or scrutiny, and that the government is not, whatever the constitution claims, 'responsible to Dáil Eireann'.

What's remarkable, however, is that this is another of what I have described elsewhere as the Irish 'unknown knowns' – things that are generally understood to be the case but whose reality we prefer to ignore. What we have instead is a system in which a basic 'truth' is established and continually referred to, even though it is patently absurd.

That 'truth' is simply stated – ministers are accountable to the Dáil for what happens in their departments. There are myths of Cuchulain and Fionn MacCumhail that have more basis in attestable fact than this. The constitution simply says nothing at all to this effect. And it never, ever happens that a minister resigns from office because of maladministration in the department that he or she theoretically heads. And yet in law (reinforced as recently as 1997) the minister *is* the department. As the Ombudsman put it in 2001, legally 'All acts of the Department and of its officials are the acts of the Minister.'

This notion that the minister *is* the department incorporates a special absurdity: the minister is not responsible for anything he or she may have said before taking up office, since he or she was not at the time that special kind of creature known as 'the Minister'. An example of this thinking was provided by Desmond O'Malley in November 1989.

O'Malley had recently become Minister for Industry and Commerce. The previous May, in opposition, he had trenchantly (and rightly) attacked the Department of Industry and Commerce for giving favourable treatment to certain firms in the beef industry. Asked in November about what he had said in May and whether he still believed it to be true, he replied that 'On May 10th "the Minister" did not say; "Deputy O'Malley" said, and that is a different matter.'⁵ To the human eye, 'the Minister' and 'Deputy O'Malley' may have worn the same blue suits, sported the same strange haircut and spoken with the same nasal snarl, but through the looking glass of Irish parliamentary accountability, they were composed of entirely 'different matter'.

Why does the transparent pretence that the minister is the flesh-and-blood incarnation of the department survive its own patent absurdity? Because it suits both ministers and civil servants. It is the perfect shield against accountability. When there is a screw-up, the senior civil servants point out that it is the minister who should answer for it to the Dáil. And the minister explains to the Dáil that he or she could not possibly have known what was happening in the bowels of the bureaucracy and that it would be absurd to blame the minister for somebody else's cock-up. Hence, in fact, nobody is answerable to anyone. The civil servants can hide behind the minister, who can hide behind the civil servants. And in spite of the ritual calls of 'Resign! Resign!', the minister gets away with it because it is genuinely absurd to expect a politician to know everything that the mandarins are up to.

There is a long history of this dodging but it reached its zenith in 2005 with the unravelling of a particularly egregious blunder. It emerged that the state had been charging elderly people for beds in public nursing homes, even though it had no legal power to do so. About €2 billion had been taken unlawfully by the state from vulnerable citizens. Who was responsible?

In 2003 the Minister for Health Micheál Martin (along with his special advisors and junior ministers) was given a briefing document that disclosed the scandal, but did nothing. Why? Because, he explained, he did not read the brief. Here is his evidence to an Oireachtas committee on the question of responsibility (the Travers report was a bland official report on the affair):

DEPUTY MCMANUS: This will cost the State a significant amount and the longer it has gone on, particularly since 2001, the more costly it has become. Who is responsible?

DEPUTY MARTIN: I accept the conclusion of the Travers Report that it was a long-term systemic corporate failure.

DEPUTY MCMANUS: Who is responsible?

DEPUTY MARTIN: I have answered.

DEPUTY TWOMEY: Is the Minister saying he is responsible?

DEPUTY MARTIN: No. I agree with the conclusions of the Travers Report, about which the committee is well aware going back to 1976.

DEPUTY TWOMEY: If so, the Minister is saying he is responsible because under the Public Service Management Act 1997, he is responsible.

DEPUTY MARTIN: The Travers Report makes a clear differentiation in terms of where he lays responsibility. He has made a determination on this and he gives the reasons, which relate to the principles, people's worries about funding and so on. He outlines ten reasons towards the end of the report. I accept that and I do not argue with his fundamental conclusions.

DEPUTY MCMANUS: I am still trying to get an answer. I asked the Minister who is responsible. Is he saying that, as Minister, he does not bear any responsibility for this?
DEPUTY MARTIN: I am, I do not.[6]

Thus, a perfect lack of accountability for what was in effect a €2 billion theft. The civil servants could not be responsible because 'all acts of the Department and of its officials are the acts of the Minister'. But the Minister 'does not bear any responsibility' because, although the civil servants briefed him, he happened not to have read the brief and could therefore plead ignorance. And, though the nursing homes scandal was a particularly spectacular case, this same system operates every day in more mundane administrative decisions that nevertheless have important consequences for individual citizens.

As the former Labour Party leader Pat Rabbitte put it in a thoughtful paper on the subject, the myth of ministerial accountability creates 'the worst of both worlds because the individual [civil servant] who made the decision is unknown and unaccountable. The person who takes notional public responsibility [the minister] is simply rubberstamping other people's decisions.'[7]

One exquisite refinement of this system is worth noting. It provides an obvious incentive to ministerial ignorance and indolence. The less a minister knows, the better. A minister who is too diligent and who reads too many briefs is placing him- or herself in the loop and is therefore potentially accountable for what is happening in the department. Micheál Martin survived essentially because he could plead 'I didn't know nothing.' In the perverse world of Irish 'parliamentary accountability', that is a good thing. This is the real 'long-term systemic corporate failure' of an illusory parliamentary democracy.

If the Dáil does not legislate and cannot hold ministers to account, what does it do? The one remaining recognisable function of a democratic parliament is to conduct inquiries on issues of public policy and the performance of state institutions. The Dáil (sometimes jointly with the Senate) does this, but in a pitifully weak way. Its one success, the Public Accounts Committee investigation into the evasion of DIRT tax by the Irish banks, was followed by a legal dismantling of the powers that allowed that investigation to be conducted. The Supreme Court ruled in 2002 that parliamentary committees could not make adverse findings against citizens. It ruled that the Dáil had 'no explicit, implicit or inherent power to conduct an inquiry'. Strikingly, Mr Justice Hardiman, in his ruling, stated that not only were citizens in general not accountable to a Dáil inquiry, but even the Garda Commissioner was 'not directly or personally responsible to the Dáil or the Oireachtas'.[8] (The case concerned an attempt by an Oireachtas committee to inquire into a police shooting at Abbeylara, County Longford in 2002.) In other words, the Oireachtas has no power to demand answers even from a senior public servant whose job it is to implement the laws it passes.

Any self-respecting parliament would have asked the people to change the constitution to reverse this decision. The Dáil did nothing. There were complaints – some of them passionate and well-argued – from some Opposition figures, but no collective desire on the part of TDs as a whole to change the constitution so as to establish their right and duty to call government departments and public institutions to account. The vast majority of TDs seemed largely indifferent to the ruling. They probably assumed that their voters didn't give a damn either. And they may have been right: Jim Mitchell, who chaired the successful DIRT inquiry, was rewarded by a grateful electorate with the loss of his seat in the 2002 election.

The limited inquiries that Dáil or Oireachtas committees can now conduct may be treated with more or less open contempt, even by State institutions. Thus, in 2010, the PAC attempted to investigate the most momentous single decision in the history of the state – the 2008 blanket bank guarantee. The Department of Finance simply refused to release fifty 'key' documents. (The term 'key' was used by the Department of Finance itself.) Some of these documents are advice from the attorney general, and could be said to be covered by legal privilege. (Though whether legal privilege should be absolute and extend to documents relating to the largest bank bailout in history is another question.)

In many cases, however, the subjects of the documents were clearly either financial or political. A 'Note to Minister re Funding situation' was not released because 'document contains confidential institution-specific information on the funding position of a particular institution'. A 'Note for Tánaiste to update Government on Financial Market Developments' was marked 'Not released – Document was submitted to Tánaiste for use at Government meeting and is subject to Cabinet confidentiality'. A 'Copy of letter from Anglo Irish Bank to the Financial Regulator' was 'Not released – confidential material received from Financial Regulator'. And so on. Essentially, civil servants were allowed to decide unilaterally which documents they should release to what is supposedly the most powerful Dáil committee, scrutinising the most expensive commitment of public money in the history of the state. How did the PAC react? It issued a statement saying it was 'somewhat disappointed'.

Why do politicians – not known, as a species, for their lack of self-regard – put up with this? One reason is the sheer debilitating burden of constituency work. As Moosajee Bhamjee, who created great excitement in 1992 when he was elected for County Clare as Ireland's first Muslim TD and then left in disillusionment after one term, put it, 'You come into the Dáil thinking that you can do this and that. But you cannot really, and constituency matters take over to a huge extent.' He found himself dealing with 'trivial things' like lighting and potholes, when he had hoped to engage in national issues such as health and education.[9] Politicians themselves are trapped in the culture of dependency they have (collectively) created – the more they feed it, the more voracious it becomes.

Another reason, of course, is the sheer amount of patronage that Irish governments have to dispense. The power of parliaments depends on the willingness of government-aligned representatives to revolt on certain issues. The tribal nature of Irish politics, with its weak commitment to ideas and its strong emphasis on group loyalty, has always discouraged this. But, just in case, governments have developed powers of patronage that an eighteenth-century constitutional monarchy would have recognised. With thirty cabinet or junior ministerial positions to be filled, committee chairmanships and vice-chairmanships to be doled out, eleven nominees to the Senate in the personal gift of the Taoiseach, promises of future preferment and threats of future vengeance to be whispered in the ear, the job of the government whips is not difficult. And with 5,000 appointments to the boards of public bodies to be handed down by government (with no parliamentary scrutiny), the network of patronage can be spread to a TD's friends and supporters.

There is a strong – and well-justified – tendency among TDs to see themselves as part of a professional, cross-party political class. National politicians are starkly unrepresentative of the population as a whole. In the last Dáil, 47 per cent of members came from the lower and higher professional classes – groups that make up just 15 per cent of the Irish population. Conversely, manual workers, who make up 10 per cent of the population, accounted for 2 per cent of TDs. The most socially deprived constituency in the country, Dublin Central, is represented by two teachers, an accountant and a professional political organiser. The Fianna Fáil minister Pat Carey has referred to the existence not just of a 'glass ceiling' in Irish politics but of a 'class ceiling' as well. Parliament, he suggested, continues to be 'the preserve of the elite few' – the legal profession, teachers and a few business people.[10]

As well as being overwhelmingly middle class, TDs as a group are much older than the general population. People aged between eighteen and thirty-five make up 28 per cent of the population but just 6 per cent of Oireachtas members.

Starker still is the under-representation of women. Just twenty-three of the 166 TDs in the current Dáil are female, and three of the most prominent, Liz McManus, Olwyn Enright and Mary Upton, have announced their intentions not to contest the next election. The situation is, if anything, getting worse. In 2007, just eighty-two of the 470 Dáil candidates were women – the lowest number since 1989. In the last local elections, just 25 per cent of candidates, and 16 per cent of those elected, were women – a reduction from the already pitiful figure of 19 per cent in the previous election. The pattern of female exclusion from the higher reaches of Irish politics has been long established. At no time in the history of the Dáil has the proportion of women TDs been higher than 14 per cent, and of the 157 people who held full ministerial positions from 1922 to 2002, only 9.6 per cent of them were women.[11]

Our system, then, gives us a parliament that does not hold governments to account, does not create laws, does not have the power to conduct serious investigations and is not representative of the people in terms either of seeking to express their views or of being at all typical of them in class, age or gender. A parliamentary system that is unable to meet any one of these basic requirements is in need of radical reform. A system that fails to meet a single one of them needs to be demolished and entirely rebuilt.

As was argued in the last chapter, change in the political system has to start with local democracy. But the creation of real local government opens the way to the creation of a real national parliament. It puts the parish pump back where it belongs – in the parish. That in turn forces the Oireachtas to clarify exactly what it is for.

For a start, with local issues handled at local level, the Dáil can be both smaller and more efficient. Exact numbers can be argued over, but it is hard to see why the Dáil needs more than 100 members. This is especially so if the Senate is to be retained. In its current form, the Senate is an utterly indefensible institution. It bears no relation even to the 'vocational' body that is envisaged in the constitution, representing different professional and social groups. It is so discredited that no one seems to care that a constitutional amendment to reform it slightly by broadening the numbers of third-level educational institutions whose graduates could vote for Senators, passed by referendum in 1979, has not been implemented.

There is, nevertheless, a good case for having a second chamber that allows those other than professional politicians to contribute to the law-making process. Such a chamber should be made up partly of representatives of the new local councils and partly of representatives of the social partners and civil society groups. It should be used, quite consciously, to make politics more representative of the population by having a requirement for gender balance and by reserving places for youth groups and religious and ethnic minorities.

As for the Dáil itself, four sweeping changes are necessary.

The first is in the electoral system. Irish people are strongly attached to the current system of proportional representation by means of the single transferable vote (STV) in multi-seat constituencies. Twice – in 1958 and 1968 – they rejected in referenda proposals by Fianna Fáil to move to a Westminster-style first-past-the-post system. And this attachment is understandable. STV is arguably the most sophisticated of voting systems. It allows the citizen to choose not just between parties but within parties – an important consideration in relation to the localism of Irish culture. It also allows them to vote against as well as for a candidate – there is a particular pleasure in working one's way down the list and placing the number 20 against the name of an especially obnoxious creep. And the end result of an STV election is, in terms of the relationship between votes cast and seats won, relatively fair.

The problem with the system, though, is that it creates intense competition within political parties. Larger parties will put up multiple candidates, especially in the larger constituencies. We know from bitter experience in Ireland that this contributes hugely to the maintenance of a clientelist culture.

One truism of Irish politics that is not mythical is that it is internal party rivalry that turns politicians into demented ward-heelers. In the Oireachtas survey, TDs themselves reported that for every extra candidate from their party in their constituency, TDs engage in higher proportions of constituency work. The factors that influence the amount of ward-heeling a TD does were found to include 'the extent to which candidates faced competition from members of their own party in the previous election, and whether a candidate had ever previously lost to a member of their own party'.

On average, a TD who faced no opponents from the same party in their constituency in 2007 spends 41 per cent of their time on constituency-related work. This figure jumps to 62 per cent for TDs who faced two or more candidates from the same party in their constituency. Those TDs who, at some point in their career, lost their seat to a fellow party member reported an average of 66 per cent of their time spent on constituency work. Interestingly, if a TD has lost their seat, but not to a fellow party member, their average level of constituency work is much lower than average, at 40 per cent. It is not war with the enemy but friendly fire that the Irish politician fears most. That fear sustains the crazy system of doling out 'imaginary patronage'. Everyone does it because, if they don't, it's sure as hell that some hungry colleague will be out on the street corners pushing the drug.

It is impossible to break this mentality without ditching the STV system, at least at national level. Since the electorate is fond of it, it can be retained for the new local governments, for which it remains appropriate. For the Dáil, the most viable alternative is probably what's called the additional member system (AMS). This is not quite as exciting as it sounds, but it does manage, on the one hand, to be fair and proportional and, on the other, to limit the degree of internal party competition.

Versions of AMS are used in Germany, New Zealand, Scotland and elsewhere. The basic idea is simple enough. About half the seats in parliament are elected in a straightforward first-past-the-post system in each constituency. But the citizen has a second vote for the other half. This is a national PR election for candidates on competing (usually party) lists. Effectively, the national list seats balance out the disproportional effect of the first-past-the-post vote. The one serious drawback of the system is that it works against independent candidates who are effectively forced to form groups in order to complete under the list system. (On the other hand, small parties can do well under the system – in Scotland, the Greens got 2 per cent of the vote in the 2010 Scottish parliament elections and the same proportion of seats: two.) But this is surely a price worth paying for the considerable benefits of greatly reducing clientelism and creating a new category of national politicians who are not dependent on constituency work.

The second essential change is one which is much easier to implement in this new electoral system – quotas for women. Quotas are at best a necessary evil. Women politicians who have been elected without them tend to resent the idea as potentially devaluing their own achievements – of the current twenty-three female TDs, fourteen are against a quota for female candidates, eight in favour and one undecided.[12] But there is absolutely no reason to believe that the grotesque imbalance in political life is going to change of its own accord. It might have seemed reasonable to expect that greater equality in the workforce and in higher education would automatically lead to a narrowing of the gap in politics. It simply hasn't happened. If anything, the position has deteriorated. In 1990 Ireland was ranked thirty-seventh in the world for the number of women in the national parliament. Now it is ranked eighty-fourth. This is either acceptable or it isn't. It seems obvious that, for a republic, it is not.

The best way to create quotas is not through complex legislation, but through financial penalties. Most of the money on which political parties run comes directly from the state. Under a list system, it is far easier for those parties to ensure that their lists (drawn up by the national organisations) are gender-balanced. Parties should get all their current state money if they have a list that is 50 per cent women. They should be docked proportionally as their number of women on the list falls below 50 per cent. Below 30 per cent and they get nothing.

The third big change that has to be made is to give Dáil and Oireachtas committees real powers to conduct inquiries. It says much about the gutlessness of so many TDs that, having gained some respect by conducting its groundbreaking inquiry into the evasion of DIRT tax by the banks, the Dáil has acquiesced in the impossibility of conducting such an inquiry ever again.

What needs to be established – preferably in the constitution – is that the Oireachtas has not merely the power but the duty to conduct inquiries for the purposes of examining the uses to which public money is being put, of holding the government of the day accountable and of scrutinising the implementation of the laws it has passed. Such inquiries by Dáil or Oireachtas committees should have the same powers and privileges as tribunals of inquiry – to compel witnesses to attend, to demand the production of all documents a committee wishes to see and to publish its findings without the risk of being sued.

The fourth crucial change is to end the charade of ministerial 'responsibility'. The system whereby ministers hide behind civil servants who hide behind ministers and no one is personally responsible for anything is at the heart of the failure of accountability in the administrative and governmental systems. As Pat Rabbitte has put it, 'The outside world is presented with the minister as personification of the department . . . Civil servants, if they appear at all, do so merely to explain and amplify upon the minister's position: there is no departmental point of view. Internally, however, the powers of the minister are capable of being exercised by any responsible officer of the department and the department is not managed by the minister but by the secretary general . . .' What holds this completely contradictory system together is an unwritten pact: 'In return for defending his department as if its actions were all his own, the minister is guaranteed that he will never walk alone and never be short of something to say in his own defence. Of course the system has one important characteristic: it can survive the imposition of even the most incompetent of ministers at its head.'

The deal, in effect, is that ministers and civil servants will collude to hide each other's incompetence. The more incompetent the minister, indeed, the happier he or she will be to act simply as a front for the department, what Rabbitte calls 'an ambassador-at-large, the Colonel Sanders for Kentucky Fried Chicken'.

How do we move beyond Colonel Sanders politics? We have to establish real transparency in the system of government, so that the name of the person who makes a decision is recorded and disclosed. Ministers should be accountable for three things: decisions they actually make, the way they follow up information they are given and the way they supervise the implementation of instructions they give to civil servants. (There are circumstances in which a minister should be held accountable for not knowing something.) Named officials should be accountable for everything else. They should be able to defend themselves when questioned – if appropriate by pointing to a minister's actions or wilful inaction. And they should take the rap when they themselves have screwed up. If it is the case that a civil servant has taken a decision in circumstances where a minister could not reasonably be expected to do so, it should be acceptable for the minister to point the finger at that civil servant. The unspoken deal whereby ministers and civil servants cover each other's behinds has to be taken off the table.

These four changes will not of themselves create a parliamentary democracy where none has existed before in Ireland. If voters still want gombeen politics, stroke-pullers and local messengers, they will get them in any conceivable electoral system. Equally, no parliament will ever transcend that culture unless it has a party system that offers voters real and serious alternatives. Those alternative ideas have to be carried into parliament by people who actually believe in them and are prepared to vote in accordance with those beliefs. Radical change does not guarantee the emergence of a functioning parliamentary democracy. But its absence certainly guarantees the survival of a dysfunctional one.

4

The Myth of Charity

Irish people, on the whole, do not regard public services as part of the package of rights and duties that defines what it means to be a citizen of a republic. They regard them as favours. At best, they come dropping 'as the gentle rain from heaven / Upon the place beneath'. At worst, you get access to them through wheedling, pleading, manipulating the system or through someone – a TD or a distant cousin who's a nun – exerting 'pull'. Why is it like this? Because of the myth of charity.

Deeply engrained in Irish culture is the idea that everything that was decent came, not from the state, but from the Church. It was not an entitlement but a blessing. Until we disentangle ourselves from this myth, we cannot begin the process of rethinking the relationship between citizens and the state that is the prerequisite for making a republic.

In June 2009 the then government chief whip, Pat Carey, said an extraordinary thing. Or, rather, a thing that is extraordinary only in Ireland. He suggested, in the context of the negotiations between the government and religious orders over the fallout from the Ryan report into systematic child abuse in Church-run industrial schools, that this might be the time for the state to 'take on its responsibilities for delivering an educational system'.

In almost every other developed society, this would be a virtually incomprehensible statement. In Ireland it is a potent one. It hints at a dawning realisation that the Ryan report was a point of no return that created the necessity for a fundamentally new deal in Church-state relations, one in which basic services in education (and in health), overwhelmingly funded by the taxpayer, finally come under public control.

To understand the need for such a new deal, it is necessary to understand why Ireland, almost alone among developed societies, allows basic social services to be run by a secretive, hierarchical organisation that has repeatedly been seen to regard itself as accountable to no one – not even to the law.

The great myth that hangs over so much discussion of the Catholic Church's domination of the education and health systems is that the Church stepped in to offer services that the state failed or refused to provide. Had it not been for the Church, the story goes, the plain people of Ireland would have been left without schools or medical services.

While there is some truth to this belief in relation to the conditions of the early nineteenth century, it is largely wrong. Indeed, the opposite is nearer the truth – the institutional Church consistently undermined state services, fought to limit their expansion and consistently put the maintenance of its own power ahead of the interests of vulnerable people.

The most spectacular case in point is the primary school system. Ireland is one of the very few countries in the developed world that does not have a national system of primary education. The church controls 2,899 of the 3,282 primary schools in the state, catering for 92 per cent of pupils. This situation didn't just happen, and nor did it arise because the Church undertook a task that the state was shirking. The overwhelming Church control of the system of primary education results, not from charity, but from the exercise of power.

In 1831 Lord E. G. Stanley, then chief secretary for Ireland, established a national schools system. A board in Dublin would make grants for the building of local schools and the payment of teachers' salaries. These schools would be under the patronage of prominent local figures. The schools would, however, be obliged to be strictly non-denominational – in the context of early nineteenth-century Ireland this meant that they would ensure equal access to Catholics, Protestants and Dissenters. The rules were that they should be managed by reputable people of both Catholic and Protestant faiths; that they should not mix religious education with basic teaching; and that they should encourage the development of religiously mixed classrooms. Religious instruction by clergy of each denomination would be separately facilitated, during special periods at the beginning or end of the school day. Pastors of all faiths would have access to the school to teach children of their own flocks during these periods. Otherwise, the curriculum would be strictly neutral.

Catholics, by and large, seemed happy with this system. They were, as one Catholic historian has pointed out, getting 'free education for the Catholic poor and the government's repeated assurances against proselytism'. (Initial opposition came primarily from Presbyterians, who burned national schools and harassed schoolmasters, and, to a lesser extent, from the Church of Ireland.)

The idea of joint Protestant–Catholic management never really took off in practice. Nevertheless, there was a reasonable level of success in establishing a public system of primary education that was, by contemporary European standards, highly progressive. On the eve of the Famine, Ireland had relatively high levels of literacy; the National Board of Education was spending £100,000 a year on primary schools; and 12,000 registered teachers were providing a basic education for half a million pupils in 4,300 schools. And the system was at least partly successful in overcoming religious segregation. In 1862 54 per cent of the primary schools throughout the island of Ireland were religiously mixed.[1]

After the Famine, however, the Catholic Church began to recreate itself as an institutional structure with power over both the civil and the intimate lives of the majority of the population. As part of that process, it set about destroying the national schools and replacing them with a specifically Catholic system. Its leader, Cardinal Paul Cullen, declared the national school system to be 'very dangerous when considered in general because its aim is to introduce a mingling of Protestants and Catholics'.

The Christian Brothers had been founded by the remarkable Edmund Rice to teach those who would not otherwise have access to education. They became, instead, the shock troops for an assault on the existing national school system. 'The Brothers' schools,' wrote the historian Barry Coldrey (himself a Christian Brother) in his seminal study *Faith and Fatherland*, 'came to be perceived by Catholic leaders as key factors in their struggle with the government for control of education in Ireland.'[2] A principal part of this strategy was that the Christian Brothers' schools (CBS) should cater not, as Edmund Rice had intended, for the destitute, but for the 'sons of the better class of the Roman Catholic population'. So far did the Brothers stray from their original mission that by the end of the nineteenth century, Archbishop Walsh of Dublin was referring to a Christian Brothers school in his diocese 'from which the poor are virtually excluded'.

There was a brilliant combination of carrot and stick.

On the one hand, the Brothers and other orders offered a Catholic and nationalist education, leavened with Victorian gentility, that was in tune with the emerging identity of the Catholic middle class. On the other, Cullen reinforced this attraction with a crude lash of spiritual intimidation. In 1869 he made an explicit threat to deny the sacraments to parents who kept their sons in 'the lion's den' of the national schools rather than send them to the Brothers.

This control of education placed the Church at the very heart of the process of modernisation in post-Famine Ireland. It was the mechanism for controlling sexuality and limiting the growth of population that had contributed to the Famine. As sociologist Tom Inglis has written, 'It was through the schools that bodily discipline, shame, guilt and modesty were instilled into the Irish Catholic. Through such discipline and control, successive generations of farmers were able to embody practices which were central to the modernisation of Irish agriculture, including postponed marriage, permanent celibacy and emigration.'[3]

The Church's campaign to destroy the mixed-denomination national schools was hugely successful. From 54 per cent in 1852, the proportion of primary schools that were religiously mixed had dropped to 36 per cent by 1900. The process of copper-fastening a sectarian system of primary education had by then become unstoppable.

The Catholic church didn't just destroy the multi-denominational national schools, it also targeted the state system of teacher education. This centred on the so-called Model Schools, which were intended to 'exhibit to the surrounding schools the most improved methods of literary and scientific instruction and to educate young persons in the office of teacher'. The schools were, as Coldrey drily notes, 'teacher training establishments outside the control of the Irish bishops'. They were also religiously mixed – in 1887, pupils at the twenty-nine Model Schools were 33 per cent Church of Ireland, 32 per cent Catholic and 27 per cent Presbyterian.

The Model Schools were destroyed by the same combination of fear and seduction that was so successful against the national schools. The fear was engendered by hellfire preaching against 'evil teaching and bad books'. The lure was the encirclement of the Model Schools by Christian Brothers establishments. Coldrey records that 'In the case of Athy, County Kildare, the Brothers were dispatched to the town at the express request of Cardinal Cullen, whose "chief object" in making this arrangement was "to counteract the godless teaching of the Model School which had been established there". The archbishop followed this action with a special ban of excommunication applied to any Catholic who sent his children to the Model School. Success attended the Brothers' efforts; within a short time not a single Catholic child was attending the Model School in Athy.'

Far from providing what the state would not, the Church increasingly set limits to the state's capacity to provide social services, whether that state was the United Kingdom or an independent Ireland. In 1892, when the UK government proposed that attendance at primary school be compulsory (a crucial protection for children who were otherwise obliged to work), the Catholic hierarchy bitterly opposed the idea as an infringement on parental rights. Partly as a result, attendance levels slipped well below international standards. In the early years of the twentieth century, daily attendance was only about 70 per cent. (To put this into context, the lowest attendance figure in Scotland, on the Orkney Islands, was 83 per cent.) The average school-leaving age in Ireland remained, at just eleven years, very low. Instead of bringing poor children into the educational system, the Church helped to keep them out.

After the foundation of the state, the Church's control of first- and second-level education became all but absolute. It not only dominated secondary schools (which remained as private, fee-paying institutions while other developed societies were making them free), but used them as recruiting grounds. Donald Harman Akenson, in his groundbreaking 1975 study *A Mirror to Kathleen's Face*, worked out that in the years 1956 to 1960, of 5,428 final-year students in diocesan colleges and secondary schools, an astonishing 1,346 professed religious vocations.

While free secondary education was becoming established as a normal aspect of a modern democratic state, Ireland continued to treat it as an essentially private and religious realm. The official Council on Education declared of secondary schools in 1960 that 'The dominant purpose of their existence is the inculcation of religious ideals and values. This central influence, which gives unity and harmony to all the subjects of the curriculum, is outside the purview of the State, which supervises the secular subjects only.'

In maintaining control of secondary schools, the Church used the same methods that had worked against the national schools. The myth is that there would have been no secondary schools without the Church. In reality, when lay people set up independent secondary schools, the Church deliberately set up in opposition to them. One small example is given by the novelist John McGahern in his *Memoir*:

A Mrs Lynch opened a secretarial school for girls in Carrick-on-Shannon; then she saw there was a need for

secondary schooling and opened the Rosary High School
for boys and girls . . . there was no secondary school for
boys in this county town. A married woman in charge
of a mixed school of adolescent boys and girls set off all
kinds of ecclesiastical alarms. Mrs Lynch must have been
a remarkable woman. The Church tried to get her to
close. She refused. They then brought in the Presentation
Brothers to close her down.[4]

The Church's dominance extended even into what was, in
theory, a non-denominational public system – that of vocational schools. As managers of primary schools, priests were
entitled to be nominated as members of the local vocational
education committees (VECs). Once on the committee, the
culture of deference virtually ensured that the priest became
chairman. In the mid-1950s, twenty-two of the twenty-seven
VECs were headed by priests.

Again, the Church's control was used not to provide services but to prevent the state providing them. Such was the
Church's determination to retain complete control of the primary school system that it actually blocked a proposal to
inject more public funds. The Irish National Teachers' Organisation (INTO) campaigned for decades for local government to pay the cost of heating and cleaning schools and for
national government to increase the state's contribution to
the capital cost of constructing them. In 1952 it was widely
expected that Sean Moylan, the then minister for education,
would finally agree to these demands. The Bishop of Clogher,
Eugene O'Callaghan, issued a strong attack on the proposals, claiming that they would lead to an 'intolerable state of
affairs whereby civil servants from Dublin might come down
and attempt to take control of the primary schools'.

When the hierarchy formally discussed the issue, its decision, according to Akenson, was 'that the present arrangements were desirable and that the school teachers should now stop their campaign'. The government dropped any move towards full funding of the primary schools. The INTO campaign petered out. Children continued to be schooled in unsuitable, badly equipped and often insanitary buildings. The anomaly whereby the state pays teachers' salaries but primary schools have to raise their own running costs continues to this day. It is a direct result of the Church's willingness to sacrifice the interests of children to the protection of its own power.

Almost equally damaging to children was the Church's resistance to the ideas of child-centred education that were emerging in developed societies throughout the twentieth century. Church control over primary education was used to insist on a punitive system. Because of original sin, children were assumed to be inclined towards badness. Thus, the Church strongly opposed the progressive educational practices of John Dewey, Maria Montessori and others that were beginning to take hold in developed societies. In 1923 Fr Denis Fahey wrote in the *Irish Ecclesiastical Review* that the educational systems of other countries had been led astray by modern theories and that 'we must return to the saner education ideal of the Middle Ages'. The archbishop of Dublin, John Charles McQuaid, condemned Montessori's theories 'wherein . . . the child is supposed to be his own end'. That punitive approach was at its most violent in the industrial school system, but it was a standard assumption of most Catholic schools.

What was true of education was almost equally true of the development of the health service. It is certainly the case that in the first half of the nineteenth century, the Church did provide medical services that were not otherwise available. (Although it is worth noting that Ireland had a long tradition of voluntary philanthropic hospitals, many of them non-sectarian in character, dating back to the early eighteenth century.) The work of orders of nuns such as the Sisters of Charity and the Sisters of Mercy was of immense value to Irish society at the time.

As the idea of public health systems began to emerge in the late nineteenth and twentieth centuries, however, the Church again successfully stymied their development in Ireland. In 1911, when David Lloyd George introduced the pioneering National Health Insurance scheme in Britain, guaranteeing free GP care and medicines for workers, the Church, allied with parts of the medical profession, successfully opposed its extension to Ireland.

The scheme would have benefited 800,000 industrial workers and domestic servants in the Irish workforce, providing them with maternity, sickness and sanatorium services as well as free access to GPs. The Catholic bishops dismissed these workers as a 'mere fraction' of the Irish population, the 'immense majority' of which, they argued, was made up of farmers or traders. They were particularly appalled that farmers, publicans and shopkeepers would be required to pay insurance for sons and daughters over sixteen who were working for them.[5] As Ruth Barrington puts it, the statement made 'no reference . . . to the needs of the increasingly desperate working class in the cities'. As usual, the Church got its way. A system that gradually became standard throughout developed Western societies was denied to Irish people. As a result, levels of public health in Ireland – including the highest rate of tuberculosis in Western Europe – remained appalling. To this day, the tangible legacy of the Church's muscle-flexing on national insurance is the system in which most patients hand over cash to their GPs at every visit.

Equally, in the 1940s and early 1950s, while the post-war world was developing national health systems, Ireland failed to do so. This was not primarily because of the state. The Department of Health produced radical proposals for a national health service in 1945. The Church, allied with right-wing doctors, opposed it on the grounds that it infringed the rights of the family. When Dr Noel Browne became minister for health in 1948, he proposed a more modest scheme under which children would have free medical care and hospitals would care for mothers before and after birth. In what became the infamous Mother and Child controversy, the Church again blocked the scheme. In all of this, the Church cemented an alliance with the top echelons of the medical profession: the Church would support the right of doctors to make very large salaries through private practice; the doctors would leave 'moral' issues (contraception, abortion, sex education, sterilisation) to the bishops. Again, there is a tangible legacy today – the godlike status and vast earnings of hospital consultants.

In health, as in education, the Church's concern was that systems of provision should remain private. The state's role should be the minimal one of supporting the provision of services for which the user would pay. Thus, in a typical disquisition, the Bishop of Cork, Cornelius Lucey, answered the question 'What should we expect from the State?': 'Help to enable us to help ourselves. Thus, instead of providing directly through its own agencies free housing for all, free health services for all, free school meals for all, etc., it should rather see to it that these are available and that people can afford to pay for them. Thus the real answer to the problem of the man who cannot afford medical care for his wife and children is not a free mother and child service for all, but a rise in wages – or cut in taxes – sufficient to enable him to pay.'

The reality is that Ireland ended up with its anomalous system of Church control in education and health, not by default, but by design. The design was the Church's determination that these services be delivered, not as the universal right of citizens, but either as gifts of its own benevolence to the very poor or as aspects of a private, market-based system for everyone else. The myth that the Church stepped into the breach to provide educational and health services because no one else would do so is entirely self-serving. The truth is that the institutional Church always put the maintenance and expansion of its own power ahead of the rights of citizens to have equal access to decent public services.

The word 'institutional' should be emphasised. Generations of committed Catholics – both lay people and those in holy orders – gave dedicated and whole-hearted service to individuals and communities in need. Some of the best civil society organisations in Ireland today – Trocaire, the Society of Saint Vincent de Paul, the Vincentian Partnership, Focus Ireland and so on – were founded by or are peopled with committed Catholics. What is at issue is not Catholicism itself or the contribution that people of faith can make to a dynamic republic. It is a very specific institution that arose from the equally specific circumstances of nineteenth-century Ireland.

That it was indeed specific is evident if we consider a whole other Irish Catholic tradition that arose at the same time – in America. In the US, Irish Catholics were in a very different situation from their co-religionists in Ireland. They were a minority within a Protestant-dominated official culture. If there were to be a fusion of Church and state in the US, the church in question would not be of the Holy, Roman and Apostolic variety. In those circumstances, the leadership of the Irish Catholic Church took precisely the opposite view to the one that became dominant at home. It argued – brilliantly and with evident sincerity – for the separation of Church and state.

In 1884 the Kilkenny-born Archbishop of Saint Paul, Minnesota, Dr John Ireland, gave a startling address to the third plenary council of the American Catholic church. It was called 'The Catholic Church and Civil Society'. Ireland, who had served as a chaplain for the Union army during the Civil War and was passionately committed to republican democracy, argued that 'the principles of the Church are in thorough harmony with the interests of the Republic'. Against the obscurantist authoritarianism of much official Catholic teaching in Europe, Ireland argued that the 'laws and institutions' of the American republic, including the constitutional separation of Church and state, were the fulfilment of the Christian vision of equality and human rights.[6] Catholics, Ireland argued, should feel 'love and admiration for the republican form of government'. Ireland's position was subsequently denounced by Pope Leo XIII as 'the Americanist heresy'. But it enabled generations of Irish Catholic women to become the driving force in the creation of the (strictly non-religious) public school system in the US. And it marks an alternative Irish Catholic tradition that is at ease with a state that upholds religious liberty by keeping its distance from any one religion.

All of this is not about the past, however: twenty-first-century Ireland is still stuck with the legacy of Church dominance of key public services. That legacy persists in both ideology and power. On the one hand, it lies in the assumption that schools and hospitals should be privately controlled entities and that their central values should be those of either the marketplace or of charity – not those of collective citizenship. On the other, it lies in the persistence of undemocratic and unaccountable power.

This power is increasingly anomalous. Church control of education and health was rooted in the realities of an almost monocultural society in which 96 per cent of people were Catholic and 91 per cent of Catholics attended Mass every week. However damaging it may have been to the idea of a republic, it had a strong basis in popular consent. This is simply no longer the case.

Firstly, only about a third of Irish Catholics can be called orthodox in the sense that they fulfil the basic obligation of weekly attendance at Mass. An *Irish Times* poll in September 2010 found just 35 per cent of Catholics claiming to attend Mass every week, with 43 per cent saying they attended 'only occasionally'. On defining issues like contraception and abortion, Catholics are increasingly unlikely to follow Church law – the vast majority use artificial contraception and support some liberalisation of the abortion laws. The assumption that all members of the Church want their children to be educated in Catholic-controlled schools is therefore increasingly dubious. Very many Catholics are entirely comfortable with the notion of a diverse and pluralist democracy in which public services are not tied to religious identity.

Secondly, Ireland is no longer a virtually monocultural society. The rise of secularism, disillusion with the Church's handling of its child abuse scandals and inward migration have broken the almost automatic link between 'Catholic' and

'Irish'. The number of Muslims rose by 70 per cent between the censuses of 2002 and 2006. Over a quarter of a million people in 2006 stated that they had no religion or declined to give a religious affiliation. Over 70,000 children under fourteen were categorised in the census as having no stated religion or belonging to a minority or non-traditional faith (i.e. not Catholic, Church of Ireland or Presbyterian). In 2007 a third of the medical and dental staff working in the Irish public health system were from minority ethnic communities.

And yet not only does the Church's institutional control remain in place, but neither of the largest political parties shows any enthusiasm for rational discussion of this fact. The power is most obvious in the education system. The Catholic Church continues to control 92 per cent of all Irish primary and secondary schools. (The religious orders that ran the horrific industrial school system continue to control over 1,000 schools between them.)

At primary level, this control is exercised through a vestige of the nineteenth-century national school system – the 'patron'. With the exception of the small but growing number of multi-denominational primary schools run by Educate Together (sixty out of 3,200 schools), the patron is almost always the local bishop. A simple question arises – if a system of primary education were being established now, would anyone in his or her right mind even think of placing them under the control of unelected, middle-aged men, accountable only to a foreign power (the Vatican)? If such a thought did arise, would it survive a moment's reflection on the inquiries into the abysmally amoral collusion of the bishops as a whole with long-term abuse of children?

Since it is rationally indefensible, the official response to continued Church control of primary education is to pretend that it is merely a matter of 'ethos' and does not constitute real power. In December 2009 the then minister for education Batt O'Keeffe told the Dáil that 'the current management of schools is working exceptionally well. The patron is in place in terms of ethos but has nothing to do with the overall management of schools. That is the responsibility of the board of management.'

This is wildly inaccurate, not least because the boards of management of primary schools are themselves both appointed by and accountable to the local bishop. The handbook given to every school principal on his or her appointment spells this out with admirable clarity: 'In appointing the board of management of the school, the bishop delegates to the members certain responsibilities for the Catholic school in the parish. Such delegation carries a duty of accountability by the board of management to the bishop and – where appropriate – to the Department of Education and Science.' (Note that accountability to the state is qualified, that to the bishop is not.)

Batt O'Keeffe misled the Dáil (presumably through sheer ignorance rather than intent) when he claimed that the role of the bishop is confined to the ethos of the school. Again the handbook is unequivocal: 'The bishop, as leader of the Catholic community in the diocese and as patron of the school, has ultimate responsibility for the school. The bishop delegates some of his responsibility to the board of management which is accountable to him. There will be contact between the board and the bishop on a number of specified issues – for instance, the appointment of the board, the appointment, suspension or dismissal of teachers, finance, school ethos.'

While the entire board of management is essentially a servant of the bishop, he has very specific powers in relation to its composition and functioning. The board's chairperson is legally obliged, according to the Constitution of Boards and Rules of Procedure issued by the Department of Education under the Education Act, to act on behalf of the bishop: 'The chairperson shall be appointed by the patron and his/her authority shall derive from such appointment.'

There is a timid suggestion in the Education Act of 1998 that the bishop in making this key appointment should 'give due consideration to the opportunity to engage in a consultative process within the wider school community'. He may, of course, consider consulting the rest of the school and decide against it, or he may consult everyone and then do what he damn well pleases.

Crucially, the bishop as patron has a legal stranglehold over the appointment and dismissal of teachers. All Catholic schools are subject to what is called Maynooth Statute 262: 'To avoid prejudice against the managership of schools, a clerical manager is forbidden to appoint any teacher or assistant, male or female, in National Schools until he shall have consulted, and obtained the approval of, the bishop: likewise a clerical manager shall not dismiss any teacher or assistant, male or female, or give notice of dismissal, until the bishop be notified, so that the teacher, if he will, may be heard in his own defence by the bishop.' Even the appointment of a special needs assistant requires the 'prior approval' of the bishop.

At both primary and secondary level, and throughout the Church-owned hospital system, Irish law still permits these bishops to dismiss any teacher, nurse, doctor or other employee who has a 'lifestyle not in keeping with the Catholic ethos'. This principle was established in 1984 in the case of Eileen Flynn, a teacher sacked in 1982 by the Sisters of Mercy in New Ross, County Wexford, because she was living with, and had become pregnant by, a married man. In the words of the nuns, 'she openly and despite warnings to the contrary continued to live a lifestyle flagrantly in conflict with the norms which the school sought to promote'. The right to dismiss employees whose lifestyle is in conflict with religious norms was upheld by the courts and copperfastened in the Employment Equality Act, which exempts from its provisions religious, educational or medical institutions under the control of a religious body.

It should be obvious that a republic cannot tolerate a situation in which publicly paid workers can be dismissed by unaccountable bishops because they are in breach of religious norms. Any openly gay or lesbian teacher or nurse, for example, is open to summary dismissal. But it is also worth noting that this regime sanctions, not religious faith, but craven hypocrisy – on the part of both the Church and its employees. The operative rule for employees is 'don't ask, don't tell'. As for the bishops and religious orders, they know very well that a majority of their female employees are not obeying one of the basic Catholic 'norms'. They are using artificial contraceptives. If they were not, the education and health systems would collapse because so many teachers, nurses and doctors would be on maternity leave. The power to dismiss employees for religious reasons is thus not a matter of principle. It is a matter of power itself, of unelected individuals holding on to an ability to threaten public workers.

In the case of non-vocational secondary education, the system is almost completely dominated by the Church, with religious orders owning the vast majority of schools. Within the vocational, theoretically public, system, religion is a core subject – pupils who do not wish to take religion classes have to leave the classroom. Most bizarrely, the tens of thousands of children who are educated at multi-denominational Educate Together primary schools do not have the option of continuing within a similar system at second level. Even in an area like the Dublin suburb of Lucan, which has five Educate Together primary schools, the organisation has not been allowed to establish a secondary school. In 2007 Educate Together applied to the Department of Education for recognition as a secondary school patron body. To date, that recognition has not been granted. After a three-year delay, the official response came in the form of the most trusted mechanism for further delay – the establishment by the minister for education in July 2010 of an expert panel, the Second-Level Patronage Advisory Group.

An even more extraordinary legacy of the Church's successful campaigns of the nineteenth-century is the stark fact that a non-Christian cannot train to be a teacher in the so-called Republic of Ireland. In December 2009 a graduate wrote to the registrar of St Patrick's College, Dublin, asking about applying for the state-funded postgraduate course in primary teaching. The qualification is from a public, non-religious institution, Dublin City University. She wrote: 'I am . . . of no particular faith and am concerned about the religious requirements for entry into a Catholic college. I am unsure if the college accepts applications from non-Catholics and would be very grateful for clarification on this issue. If this is the case, I would also be grateful for clarification on whether it is obligatory for non-faith students to complete the diploma in religious education and teach religion as part of their teaching practice.' The reply assured her that non-Catholics could indeed apply, but stressed that 'students on the course are required to take all the programme modules and these include modules on religious education in primary schools'.

The solution, you might think, would be to apply to another teacher-training course. The fact is, though, that every single course in Ireland is run by a Christian college, and obliges every single student to both learn and teach Christian doctrine. There are seven teacher training colleges, all of them funded by the state. St Patrick's defines itself as a 'community of learning in which Catholic religious values and equity are promoted'. It adds that 'the college recognises its duty in preparing teachers to teach the Catholic faith in Catholic schools'. Mary Immaculate College in Limerick declares itself on its website to be 'Ireland's largest Catholic college'. Froebel College in Dublin defines itself as a 'Catholic College, under the trusteeship of the Congregation of Dominican Sisters'. St Angela's in Sligo declares itself 'a Catholic college'. The Marino Institute in Dublin is run by the Christian Brothers and declares itself committed to the tradition of that order's founder, Edmund Rice. And the Church of Ireland College of Education is explicitly dedicated to providing 'a supply of teachers for primary schools under the management of the Church of Ireland and other Protestant denominations'.

These colleges are not private institutions – each is connected to a public university and each is run with public money. Yet in all of them, students have no choice but to learn (and pass exams in) Christian doctrine. (Two colleges offer optional courses for those who wish to teach in Educate Together schools, but these are in addition to, rather than instead of, the compulsory Catholic courses. These courses are taken by 50 of 2,400 students – accounting for 0.0016 per cent of state spending on primary teacher education.)

The religious education part of the course is specifically designed to enable the teaching of the 'textbooks currently in use in Irish Catholic schools'. Students are required to 'explore some of the theoretical foundations of contemporary faith formation processes' – in other words, to learn how to indoctrinate children in the Catholic faith. When it comes to teaching practice, the curriculum in St Patrick's stipulates that 'it is expected that all students would prepare religion lessons'.

Again, the government of the Republic chooses neither to defend nor deny this effective closure of an entire public sector profession – primary teaching – to anyone who is not, or is not prepared to pretend to be, a believing Catholic or member of the Church of Ireland. It simply pretends that there is not a problem. Asked what provision is made for non-Christian students, the then minister, Batt O'Keeffe, told the Dáil that 'responses received from some colleges in relation to the question of provision being made for student teachers who belong to a denomination which is not Christian have indicated that this has not arisen to date'.

The logic is impeccable: you have to pretend to be a Christian to train as a teacher – therefore all trainee teachers are assumed to be Christians. Subsequently, Labour TD Seán Sherlock asked Minister of State at the Department of Education Conor Lenihan to state in the Dáil 'the provision that is made in each of the colleges of education for students who object on grounds of religious belief or non-belief or other grounds of conscience to participating in faith formation'. He also asked whether 'there is any recognised and viable education and career path open' to such people. Lenihan's answer was that 'The bachelor of education courses provided by the colleges of education include compulsory modules on religious education . . . There is no separate qualification for primary teaching available in the State which does not include religious education . . . My department asked the colleges of education whether a student has ever objected on grounds of religious belief or non-belief or other grounds of conscience to participating in faith formation . . . The responses received from the colleges so far have indicated that this has not arisen to date.' This is the official view of blatant religious discrimination in state-funded institutions – it is simply not an issue.

Indeed, Irish law specifically protects the right of both schools and colleges of education to discriminate on religious grounds. While the constitution states that 'the State guarantees not to endow any religion' and 'shall not impose any disabilities or make any discrimination on the ground of religious profession, belief or status', this is treated as so much pious republican verbiage. The Employment Equality Act of 1998 specifically allows training colleges for primary teachers to discriminate on religious grounds in their admissions policies. It also allows both hospitals and schools to discriminate on the grounds of religion in employment. Likewise, the Equal Status Act of 2000 specifically allows primary and secondary schools to discriminate on religious grounds in deciding who to admit as a pupil.

The Church seeks to justify the persistence of this nineteenth-century system on two grounds. One is that it is a result of popular choice. The argument is circular – most parents have no choice but to send their children to Catholic schools, therefore most parents choose Catholic schools. In fact, support for the current system has collapsed, both internally and externally. More than 80 per cent of primary teachers believe the Catholic Church should relinquish control of some or all of its schools.[7] An *Irish Times* poll in January 2010 found that 61 per cent of respondents believed that the Catholic Church should give up its control of the primary school system, with just 28 per cent supporting the status quo.[8]

As a fallback position, therefore, the Church has adopted a crude appeal to multiculturalism. Because the term has been lazily used in the context of immigration into Ireland, it has a liberal gloss. It is, however, an essentially reactionary notion that envisages citizens being locked in to various static identities, usually arranged around one dominant mainstream. For the hierarchy, however, it serves a purpose. Church domination of the education system can be seen as an expression, no longer of power, but rather of identity. The Church now purports to favour a kind of 'pluralism' – not within schools, but among schools. All parents will have the right to send their children to schools that reflect their own individual identities.

This may sound attractive, but it is neither desirable nor practical. The idea of balkanising the school system (and by implication the hospital system) into any number of 'identity' groups in which every religious, ethnic or ideological category can be separately educated is a terrible grounding for democratic citizenship. (The state, of course, could have no grounds for denying to Scientologists or Jedi the provisions it makes for Catholics or Muslims.) But it is also ludicrously expensive. Even at the height of its economic boom, Ireland could never have afforded to build and maintain multiple schools in every significant centre of population. The idea that it could do so in a long period of austerity is either disingenuous or deluded.

The Church's institutional power is nothing more than a

historic dead weight. It neither can nor should be sustained. The real question is whether it is dealt with through a long and sterile war of attrition between 'secularists' and 'traditionalists' or whether the chance to shrug off that dead weight becomes a stimulus for the invention of a real republic. If the first option is taken, Ireland will be saddled with yet another expenditure of collective energy on pointless irrelevancies. If the second road is travelled, the consequent process of thinking about citizenship can be exciting and liberating. This does not have to be a zero-sum game. It is possible for almost everyone to win.

That most certainly includes Irish Catholicism. The reality is that the accumulation of temporal power has been, in the long-term, a disaster for the Irish Church. Its stifling 'moral monopoly' – its ability to dominate collective thought processes through the education system and to marginalise dissent – made it lazy and intellectually weak. It developed no intellectual immune system and was thus unable to deal with the more critical environment of secular modernity. More importantly, it became, not a radical challenge to the values of a self-satisfied society, but the bulwark of that self-satisfaction. Contrary to the instincts and desires of so many active Catholics, it became trapped in the reactionary posture of an Establishment that had nothing to gain by change and everything to lose. The grotesquely corrupting effects of its power are smeared across the pages of the Ryan and Murphy reports.

Dismantling that institutional power could liberate the Church into its proper sphere – that of civil society. There is a vast field of voluntary and community activity to which people of faith can, and do, bring energy and a sense of purpose, as well as a humility and concern for human dignity.

Irish society, as well as the Church, can benefit hugely from the release of those energies.

Equally, the process of thinking about new structures for the ownership, control and ethos of what are currently Church-dominated systems will be a great stimulus to genuinely democratic thinking. It is clear, for example, that while most Irish people don't want the Church to control primary schools, they don't want the state, in a crude sense, to do so either. Indeed, the most effective rhetorical argument put forward by Church leaders is, 'Yes, but do you want all your schools run by civil servants in Dublin?' The answer, clearly, is no.

How should they be run, then? Locally and democratically. It is not difficult to construct a system of primary education that reverts to the original idea of the national schools, with a core curriculum that occupies the basic school day and facilities provided for optional religious instruction. (The Educate Together schools already have such a system and it runs to the satisfaction of all the religious groups involved.) Ownership and control are more difficult questions, and therefore, in a sense, more exciting ones. They involve actually working out how democratic citizenship should function in Ireland – a question we have avoided throughout our history.

Control is, at least in principle, simple enough: schools should be run democratically by elected representatives of the parents, the staff, the local community and, in the case of secondary schools, the pupils. What would be interesting in the transition from a sectarian to a non-sectarian system, though, is that those representatives could no longer be assumed to share an 'identity'. All they would share is their common citizenship and membership of a community. The process of using those commonalties to run a public service would be an education in practical republican democracy.

As for ownership, the obvious place for it to be vested is with local governments. Successful educational systems all over Europe are run by local councils. The problem – and the opportunity – is that Ireland has nothing like a system of local government that would be adequate to the task. Taking democratic control of education demands a complete reinvention of local government. In the lazy mindset of official thinking, that is a very good reason not to do it. In a serious renewal of Irish democracy, it is an excellent reason to embrace the opportunity. Primary schools are arguably the public institutions most intimately entwined with the everyday lives of families and communities. If we could create collective democratic systems in which we could trust ourselves – rather than a bishop appointed by Rome – with the ownership of those institutions, we would be some way down the road to creating a real republic.

There is one other challenge involved in moving beyond the legacy of nineteenth-century Church power. It is the challenge of values. Through its control of schools and hospitals, the Church has been able to define the 'ethos' of some of the most crucial public services. That ethos may have appeared firm and certain. In reality, with the exception of a narrow range of issues to do with sexuality and reproduction, it has become increasingly fuzzy. It has embraced, for example, commitments to social justice and equality on the one side, and expensive private education for the rich on the other. It has embraced an ethic of service to all on the one side, and the construction of private for-profit hospitals on the other. And these contradictions have fed into the slipperiness of Irish public policy, encouraging its tendencies to adopt both sides of every argument.

But if the 'ethos' is no longer to be that of the Church, whose is it to be? The process of ending Church control in education and health is one that demands the articulation of a new public morality. In the case of schools or hospitals, it demands a collective ability to answer the basic questions of what they are for and by what values and priorities they should be organised. A society that can actually answer those questions might begin to deserve the name of a republic.

5

The Myth of Wealth

Even as they become poorer, Irish people have a tantalising memory of a golden age when Ireland was one of the richest countries in the world. Like all golden ages, this one is a figment of the imagination.

In 2007 Bank of Ireland Private Banking declared Ireland the second richest nation in the developed world, after Japan. For Irish people raised on misery and misfortune, the figures were dazzling. The bank's bar chart showed the thrusting, phallic bar for 'net wealth per head' in Ireland pushing over the €160,000 mark. The relatively virile United States was just past €120,000. The poor, flaccid Germans extended only to €100,000. And the Canadians, for all their frontier ruggedness, couldn't get their graph to rise beyond €90,000.

These figures ought to have been patently ludicrous. It was obviously true that Ireland had become much wealthier than it had ever been before. The marks of money were everywhere, from the size of the houses that were selling as fast as the Polish and Lithuanian workers could build them, to the frenzied prices that were being charged – and paid – for everything from cups of coffee to designer handbags. But did anyone seriously believe that the Irish were 60 per cent richer than the Germans? If these figures were real, Germany was now as far behind Ireland in terms of per capita wealth as

Ireland had been behind Germany in the 1980s. Perhaps the Irish should have been doing for the Germans what the German taxpayers had been doing back then – subsidising the building of roads and sewerage in the Ruhr valley.

Yet the idea that the Celtic Tiger had turned Ireland into one of the two or three wealthiest nations on earth was almost a commonplace of the boom years. And it seemed to be a self-fulfilling prophecy. In 2002, Dan McLaughlin, Bank of Ireland's chief economist declared that 'By 2005, Ireland will only be surpassed by Luxembourg as the richest country in the world.'[1] The apogee of this absurdity was reached in September 2010 when, with Ireland drowning in debt, the Central Statistics Office was still declaring it, on the basis of GDP, the second richest country in the EU.

Ireland's status as the national equivalent of a Russian oligarch or a Saudi oil sheik was always illusory. It was a trick of statistics and wishful thinking. And this matters now because Ireland's future depends on a radical reappraisal of our understanding of what it means to be wealthy. If we hold in our heads the ideal of the boom years as a period of stunning prosperity, we will not understand why the boom failed. More fatally, we will be trying to 'return' to a place we never really were.

What happened in Ireland in the first boom of 1995 to 2001 was a process of catching up. Ireland had been what the *Economist* called in 1988 'the poorest of the rich' – a beggar that had somehow slipped in to the gentleman's club of the European Community. Its GDP per capita was just two-thirds of the EC average. In the 1990s, through a combination of social change, intelligent policies and sheer good fortune, Ireland became what it ought to have been – a typically prosperous Western European economy.

As the boom went into overdrive in the new millennium, however, it suited almost everyone to hype up this success. For the right (both domestically and internationally), it was useful to point to Ireland's spectacular growth as proof that low taxes and light-touch regulation had magical effects. For the left, on the other hand, it was rhetorically beneficial to point to continuing examples of social squalor and poverty and ask 'How can this be allowed to continue in the second richest country in the world?'

This canopy of myth was held up by three pillars of il-lusion – the statistical quirks of GDP; the identification of wealth with income; and the ignoring of both the burden of debt and the cost of living.

For most countries, Gross Domestic Product (national output) and Gross National Product (national income) are more or less interchangeable. This is not the case for Ireland. Because the Irish economy is uniquely dependent on trans-national corporations, who tend to inflate their earnings in Ireland to take advantage of low corporation tax rates, and who then repatriate profits and royalties, GDP significantly overstates real living standards. Typically, in Europe during these years, the gap between the two figures was about 0.3 per cent. In Ireland, it was 25 per cent. Everyone knew this – but almost everyone preferred to use the flattering and unreal GDP figures to compare Ireland to the rest of the world.

In 2002, for example, Ireland's GDP per head of population was almost $34,000 – a mightily impressive figure. But GNP per capita was almost $27,000 – still a very good number but not nearly so spectacular. In 2005, when the idea of Ireland being 'the second richest country in the world' took hold, Ireland's real income per capita (measured by GNP) was just below the average of the developed OECD economies, slightly above the average of the European Union's fifteen old members, and equivalent to the sixth poorest state in the US. And by 2010 Ireland, measured by GNP per capita, was actually below the OECD average. In GDP terms, Ireland was ranked ninth of twenty-eight OECD countries. If GNP was used instead, the ranking fell to eighteenth.[2]

It has to be borne in mind that, throughout the boom years, Ireland was enjoying a huge demographic bonus compared to its Western European neighbours. The bulk of its population was of working age, with relatively few retired people. The so-called 'dependency ratio', which measures the number of people over sixty-five relative to the number of working age, tells the story. Ireland's was 17.4 per cent in 2007, compared with the OECD average of 26 per cent. This alone boosted per capita income. When this factor is taken into account, and GNP is used instead of GDP, Irish wealth in the boom years ceases to look so dazzling.

Even without the distorting mirror of GDP, however, Ireland's self-image as a super-rich state would have been seriously delusional. Income – especially national income – is not wealth. The Irish, in fact, had more reason than most to be sceptical of crude notions of collective 'wealth'. Ireland had previously been part of the 'richest country in the world'. It was called the United Kingdom. At the time of the UK's global ascendancy, Ireland experienced what was proportionally the deadliest famine in known world history and suffered a catastrophic decline in its population through mass emigration. Even if it were true that boomtime Ireland was actually richer than Germany, it would not have followed that the place was in great shape.

Real national wealth is accumulated over many generations and manifests itself in fixed assets, public services, infrastructure (both physical and social) and capacity for innovation. The Celtic Tiger did not make Ireland rich by any of these measures.

On the surface Ireland experienced a phenomenal growth in the value of fixed assets, which more than doubled from €222 billion in 2000 to €477 billion in 2008. The problem is that most of this growth was accounted for by housing, which accounted for over €300 billion of the total. If we take housing out of the equation, the real growth in fixed assets was just €70 billion. A large chunk of this – €20 billion – was in retail infrastructure like warehouses and shops.

In fact, over those eight years, the balance between economically productive assets and unproductive ones shifted dramatically in the wrong direction. In 2000, the unproductive capital stock was worth €14 billion more than the productive. By 2008, the gap had grown to €118 billion.[3] And most of the productive investment in fixed assets was made by the state (roads, rail, water, sewerage, schools, hospitals and so on). Private firms put just €17 billion into the pot – a figure described by Davy's Stockbrokers economist Rossa White as 'pathetic'. Private sector productive capital stock grew by just 26 per cent in eight years, a miserable figure for an economy in the midst of the greatest boom in its history. The result is that indigenous firms continued to lag far behind the transnational corporations that dominated the economy. Foreign-owned companies accounted for almost 90 per cent of total Irish exports in 2008.

This imbalance is reflected in the nature of private wealth in Ireland in the boom years. Property (residential and commercial) was by far the dominant form of wealth, accounting for 72 per cent of all assets.[4] Of the €804 billion in 'wealth' (net assets) enjoyed by Irish households at the end of 2006,

€671 billion was accounted for by residential property. Those houses were worth, to be optimistic, about half of what they were being valued at – a €335 billion hole in Irish 'wealth'.

The problem is all too obvious in the new Ireland of negative equity and Nama – you don't get rich by buying very expensive houses. If we look at financial assets – as opposed to either income or the supposed value of property – a more realistic picture of the wealth of Irish households emerges. In 2005 the total financial assets of households in the Netherlands and the UK were around 300 per cent of those countries' GDP. In Ireland total household financial assets were 169 per cent of GDP or 200 per cent of GNP.[5] Perhaps more telling are the figures for household financial assets as a percentage of net disposable income – a measure that takes into account outgoings like mortgage payments. In the Netherlands and Belgium financial assets were over 360 per cent of disposable income. In Ireland they were 164 per cent.

Even before we look at public services or the quality of life, it is starkly evident that the boom left Ireland a remarkably poor place by many of the basic economic criteria for developed economies.

Infrastructure is poorly developed. Even in 2010, after significant investment for the previous decade, a survey of international executives ranked Ireland twenty-sixth of twenty-eight OECD countries for infrastructure. In each of the four categories – air transport, distribution networks, water and energy – Ireland's ranking was below twenty. Forfás sums up the deficit: 'There are significant weaknesses in terms of broadband speeds, distribution infrastructure, public transport and cycle lanes, water and waste infrastructure and natural gas storage capacity.'

Broadband is one of the most obvious areas of economic

poverty. A higher proportion of fixed connections (31 per cent) are slower than 2 mb/s than in any comparable country. In the eurozone as a whole, 20 per cent of connections are faster than 10 mb/s. In Ireland, just 9 per cent are. In Portugal the figure is 61 per cent; in Belgium 41 per cent and in Denmark 35 per cent. In Ireland just 0.6 per cent of broadband connections are over fibre optic cables, compared to 51 per cent in Japan, 46 per cent in South Korea and 21 per cent in Sweden.

In terms of energy and transport, Ireland remains deeply underdeveloped. Sustainable energy production and efficient transport are increasingly important forms of national wealth. The use of oil – all of it imported, of course – in Ireland more than doubled between 1990 and 2008, while the use of gas rose by 210 per cent. Ireland was consuming 50 per cent more oil for transportation per head than the European Union average.[6] Ireland is the ninth most oil-dependent society in the world. In the Siemens/Economist Intelligence Unit European Green City Index at the end of 2009, Dublin ranked thirtieth of thirty cities.

Instead of tackling this profound problem, government policy during the boom years made it far worse. Bad planning and the property bubble encouraged people to live further and further from their places of work. The government's Transport 21 plan proposed to spend five times as much on roads as on rail. (Average peak-hour traffic speed in Cologne in 2002 was 40 km per hour; in Helsinki it was 36 and in Belfast it was 27. In Dublin it was 16.5.) The proportion of overall energy use that came from renewable sources increased merely from 2.3 per cent in 1990 to 3.9 per cent in 2008.[7] This is half the OECD average – this for a country with huge natural advantages in wind and tidal power. Ireland ranks twenty-second of twenty-eight OECD countries for renewable energy and twenty-first for control of carbon emissions.

In an era when environmental sustainability has at last been understood to be a form both of present prosperity and of real wealth for the future, the legacy of Ireland's boom has been a bleak impoverishment. On an index aggregating twenty-five environmental indicators relating to health, air quality, water resources, productive natural resources, bio-diversity and habitat, sustainable energy and climate change, Ireland is ranked twentieth of twenty-eight OECD countries.

What is true of the physical infrastructure is also true of significant parts of the social and intellectual infrastructure. Two good ways of measuring the productive intellectual capital of a country are research and development and product innovation. Irish R&D expenditure as a percentage of GNP was 1.7 per cent in 2008 – below the OECD average. The number of researchers per thousand people employed in Ireland in 2008 was six, substantially below the OECD average of 8.5. The contribution of innovative activity to the turnover of Irish firms was below the eurozone average and actually fell between 2006 and 2008. In terms of international patents granted to firms, Ireland is well below the OECD average, ranking seventeenth of twenty-eight countries.

Of the twenty-five most developed OECD countries ranked for 'human and income poverty' by the United Nations Development Programme in 2009, Ireland was placed twenty-third. (The rankings are in inverse order – the higher the rank the better.) Sweden, Norway, the Netherlands, Denmark and Finland were at the top. Ireland was sandwiched between the United States and Mexico. The only European country with a worse ranking was Italy.

Much social infrastructure, even after the boom years,

remained at levels that would have shocked citizens of ostensibly much poorer countries. A few random examples of primary schools illustrate the point. The primary school in Julianstown, County Meath, has 70 per cent of its pupils in prefabs (some more than twenty-five years old), just four of the thirteen classrooms meeting national standards, nowhere for parents and teachers to meet privately, mouse-traps in every room and toilets 'from another era', their smell 'permeating the classrooms'.[8] Eglish primary school was described by its principal as a 'rat-infested fire-trap' in which children were endangered by slates falling off the roof.[9] The primary school in Ballinakillen, County Carlow, was described by the local priest as reminiscent of scenes from *Slumdog Millionaire*, with black mould growing on the walls and fifty-seven pupils in one prefab 'that reeks of urine'. Teachers invented stories to explain away the sounds of rats scurrying under the floorboards.[10] In 2008, when Ireland was at its 'richest', 2,253 prefabs were in use in primary schools throughout the country – meaning that around 50,000 children were being educated in glorified sheds. (For the privilege, €160 million of their parents' taxes was spent on renting these prefabs from private owners between 2006 and 2009.)

Within parts of the public health system, the squalor was even more degrading. Orla Tinsley, an eighteen-year-old woman with cystic fibrosis, caused widespread shock in 2005 when she wrote in the *Irish Times* about the conditions she had to endure in the national referral centre for the disease, St Vincent's Hospital in Dublin. Suffering from a condition in which common infections could kill her, she had spent two nights in A&E next to patients with the MRSA superbug, before being placed in a geriatric ward with severely disturbed and incontinent patients. Five years on, she reported being in the same hospital and having to share a room with 'five other women on a ward where the staff did not specialise in cystic fibrosis'.[11] To reach international standards, Ireland needed a unit with thirty-four beds for cystic fibrosis patients. It was not 'rich' enough to build one.

The former inspector of mental hospitals, Dr Dermot Walsh, said that he 'cringed and shivered' at the thought of colleagues from abroad seeing the living conditions of some Irish psychiatric patients.[12] The official Mental Health Commission report for 2009 uses the word 'unacceptable' eight times in relation to such conditions – in one case using the phrase 'entirely unacceptable and inhumane'. The inspector of mental hospitals found 'no discernible overall improvement in standards' that had long been reported as humiliating for patients.

St Brendan's in Dublin had a female ward in a nineteenth-century building that was 'unfit for purpose'. 'Many residents were wandering around the unit on the day of inspection, apparently aimlessly . . . The atmosphere generated on the unit due to the mix of residents and lack of space, was tense and stressful for both residents and staff.' At St Ita's, also in Dublin, the inspector found 'two large unsuitable dormitories, toilets that lacked privacy, and showers that had mould and staining . . . 125 people lived in sub-standard accommodation and the admission units remained unfit for purpose.' In June 2010 three major public mental hospitals – St Senan's in Wexford as well as St Brendan's and St Ita's – were forced to stop admitting patients because they could not meet minimal standards of care.

At the level of individuals and families, there was a similar mismatch between delusions of grandeur and more mundane realities. Near full employment and low taxes certainly created a sense of prosperity. Most people, however, were not earning astronomical wages – in 2006, two-thirds of all employees were earning less than €20 an hour, and 14 per cent were earning less than €10 euro an hour. If you were childless, in good health, had a decent job and didn't buy an overpriced house, the low taxes of boomtime certainly helped you to feel affluent. Even for those who were not unfortunate enough to have children or to be ill or dependent on public provision, however, Irish wealth was often much more illusory than real. The Celtic Tiger model was very good at putting money into people's pockets through low taxation. But it was also very good at taking it out again through the need to pay for services that most Europeans received as part of their social contract with the state.

A European Commission report in 2008 showed Ireland with the lowest public spending on childcare and early childhood education. The other side of this equation was that parents in Ireland spent the second highest proportion of their net income (after the UK) on childcare. Whereas in countries like Belgium and Portugal parents spent less than 5 per cent of their income on childcare, in Ireland the figure was close to 30 per cent.[13] In Spain the monthly bill for keeping two children in a crèche (after public subsides) was €330. In Ireland it was almost €2,000.

Healthcare tells a similar story. For those without medical cards (essentially everyone except pensioners and welfare recipients), GP visits have to be paid for – at a cost of €50 to €70 a time. (Over half of adults reported avoiding visits to their GP because of the expense.) At the height of the boom in 2008, 2.3 million people in Ireland (53 per cent of the population) had private health insurance cover – largely because of fears about timely access to the public health system. The Health Insurance Authority noted that 'the important determinants of demand for private health insurance in Ireland' included 'the existence of waiting lists for elective treatment in the public hospital system and perceptions among the public of better care being available for private patients'.[14] These people, according to the HIA's surveys, 'see private health insurance as a necessity, not a luxury, which brings peace of mind'.

The price that customers paid for this insurance rose rapidly during the boom years: the largest company, Voluntary Health Insurance (VHI), typically increased its charges by 9 per cent a year, but in 2002–3 inflicted a whopping 18 per cent rise on its members. In addition to these costs, large numbers of people also took out other forms of health cover – 33 per cent of those with health insurance also had serious illness insurance to provide lump-sum cash payments, 31 per cent had income protection against ill health and 21 per cent had health cash plans to provide payments during hospital treatment. Fear of not being able to get access to treatment or of being impoverished by ill health cost Irish people dear. Some people ended up paying for healthcare in four different ways – through taxation for the public system, through fees for GP visits and consultations with specialists, through private health insurance and through extra insurance schemes.

Primary and secondary education, supposedly 'free', are in fact very expensive. Three quarters of primary school parents make a 'voluntary' contribution to basic running costs like lighting, heating and maintenance.[15] In nearly a third of primary schools, parents have to raise more than €10,000 a year just to cover basic costs. At secondary level, schoolbooks, which are free in almost every Western European country, cost hundreds of euro for every child every year.

When costs like schoolbooks, uniforms, sports gear, stationery and administrative charges are added in, most parents end up paying in the region of €1,000 per child per year for a 'free' secondary education.

The biggest extra cost of Ireland's neo-liberal economic model, though, was in housing. During the boom, the government almost stopped the provision of social housing while encouraging a rampant frenzy of private house building. In 1975 local authorities constructed 33 per cent of all new housing in Ireland. During the boom years of 1995 to 2007 this shrunk to just 6 per cent.[16] This collapse in public provision had huge hidden costs for private house buyers. Public housing provision had helped to control the property market. The abandonment of that control helped to make housing in Ireland crazily expensive. Average new house prices in Dublin increased by over 400 per cent between 1994 and 2007. The price of second-hand houses rose by 500 per cent.

Inevitably, the cost of this housing also rose enormously as a proportion of incomes. People may have felt wealthy during the boom years – their average earnings rose by 70 per cent between 1995 and 2007. But if they aspired to own a house (which most Irish people do), this 'wealth' was swallowed up. Seventy per cent ceases to look all that great when set against a 350 to 500 per cent rise in the cost of a house – and, of course, of a mortgage. The average value of a mortgage rose from €62,000 in 1997 to €270,218 in 2008.

The cost of mortgages, in turn, was the biggest single factor in the final crack in Ireland's facade of wealth – debt. The 'richer' Ireland got, the more the Irish owed. Household debt doubled in just five years between 2004 and 2009.[17]

By 2009 Irish households were among the most indebted in the world. Household borrowing in Ireland was over 100 per cent of GNP – twice the equivalent figure in the eurozone as a whole. Household debt as a percentage of disposable income increased from 48 per cent in 1995 to approximately 176 per cent in 2009. Ireland's household debt per capita peaked at €37,464 in 2008 (at that point Irish households were paying out €9.3 billion a year in interest on loans – almost 10 per cent of their disposable income). At the start of 2010 Irish households owed €110 billion in mortgages and €24 billion in consumer loans. And household debt was merely a part of overall private sector debt, which, by September 2009, stood at 290 per cent of GNP.

Given the ludicrous bar charts showing the Irish to be 60 per cent more wealthy than the Germans, it is rather ironic that the illusion of Irish wealth was partly created by the swamping of the country in a tide of German money. While frugal German savers were building up huge deposits in their banks, those banks were anxious to lend. The Irish banks were happy to oblige them by borrowing as fast as the money could be shovelled out to property developers and mortgage holders. In December 2009 figures from the Bundesbank showed that German banks were owed €32 billion by Greek banks and €165 billion by Spanish banks. They were owed €174 billion by Irish banks.

In all of this, Ireland became a perfect exemplar of what Colin Crouch has called 'privatised Keynesianism'. When the original boom petered out in 2002, the government, addicted as it was to a crude neo-liberal ideology, was never going to use classic Keynesian counter-cyclical polices to boost the flagging economy. Instead, like governments in the other Anglo-Saxon economies, it turned consumers into millions of mini-Keynesians. As Crouch puts it, 'Under original Keynesianism, it was governments that took on debt to stimulate the economy. Under the privatised form individuals, particularly poor ones, took on that role by incurring debt on the market . . . In addition to the housing market there was an extraordinary growth in opportunities for bank loans and credit card debt . . . Bad debts were funding bad debts, and so on in an exponentially growing mountain.'[18] Ireland had plenty of these ragged-trousered Keynesians. In 2006, at the height of the boom, 9 per cent of the Irish population experienced debt problems arising from everyday expenses.

Taken together, the exaggerations of GDP, the poverty of fixed assets, the personal costs of weak public services, the illusory nature of property values and the swamp of debt undermine the idea that Ireland, even in the boom years, was seriously rich. And this in turn should raise basic questions about the nature of future prosperity. There is still, in the minds of many in the political establishment and the ranks of right-wing economists, a notion that what has happened to Ireland is an unfortunate accident in an otherwise successful economic model. Some of the driving got a bit reckless, and there was an inevitable crash, but the car itself is still sleek and powerful. With new safety belts and air bags, it will take us back on the road to consumer heaven.

In fact, the Irish experience of the last fifteen years suggests that we need to think again about what constitutes real wealth. Phenomenal growth rates did not, in Ireland, produce either top-class systems of health, education and housing, cutting-edge public infrastructure or sustainable prosperity. The lesson is surely one that chimes with an insight that has been gaining ground in the last few years – the utter inadequacy of GDP or GNP as measures of increasing (or decreasing) levels of well-being in a society.

In 2008 the French president Nicholas Sarkozy asked the

economists Joseph Stiglitz, Amartya Sen and Jean Paul Fitoussi to establish a commission to consider the limits of GDP as a measure of economic and social progress. This was a recognition that ideas of measurement are not merely abstract: 'What we measure affects what we do; and if our measurements are flawed, decisions may be distorted. Choices between promoting GDP and protecting the environment may be false choices, once environmental degradation is appropriately included in our measurement of economic performance. So too, we often draw inferences about what are good policies by looking at what policies have promoted economic growth; but if our metrics of performance are flawed, so too may be the inferences that we draw.'[19]

As the commission pointed out, 'traffic jams may increase GDP as a result of the increased use of gasoline, but obviously not the quality of life'. This echoes the point made by the New Economics Foundation: 'The revenues skimmed off the financial system by traders in the City of London as the pyramid of "toxic" derivatives was being built added to GDP; cleaning up the effects of pollution increases GDP; paying the costs of high rates of crime increases GDP. None of these things can be said to build lasting social or environmental value. Rather, they are highly destructive of it.'[20] Famously, a couple that stays married does not thereby add to GDP. A couple that divorces boosts GDP by paying fees to lawyers and setting up new households.

Even in terms of its basic aim of measuring production of goods and services, GDP is good at measuring quantity but not quality. GDP is also particularly misleading in unequal societies: 'If inequality increases enough relative to the increase in average per capital GDP, most people can be worse off even though average income is increasing.'

Much of what the commission had to say about the role of inadequate ways of measuring wealth in the global economic crisis is especially relevant to Ireland: 'Neither the private nor the public accounting systems were able to deliver an early warning, and did not alert us that the *seemingly* bright growth performance of the world economy between 2004 and 2007 may have been achieved at the expense of future growth. It is also clear that some of the performance was a "mirage", profits that were based on prices that had been inflated by a bubble.'

To avoid a recurrence of the same delusion, we need a 'timely and complete set of wealth accounts – the "balance sheets" of the economy – that could give a comprehensive picture of assets, debts and liabilities of the main actors in the economy.' The liabilities have to include the depletion of non-renewable resources and damage to the environment that creates short-term profits at the expense of long-term impoverishment.

The key message of the commission is that 'the time is ripe for our measurement system to *shift emphasis from measuring economic production to measuring people's well-being'*. It identifies the basic criteria by which well-being should be measured as 'material living standards (income, consumption and wealth); health; education; personal activities including work; political voice and governance; social connections and relationships; environment (present and future conditions); and insecurity, of an economic as well as a physical nature'.

The ways of making this shift may be complex and technical (the commission's template is the obvious place to start) but the basic idea is actually increasingly familiar to millions of Irish people in their daily lives. Every time a politician talks about 'turning the corner' or an economist talks about 'returning to growth', people who see the dole queues lengthening and their own real standards of living diminishing know exactly the difference between a measure based on raw growth and one based on actual human lives. The gap between one and the other is also the gap between official delusions and lived experience.

The aim of change would not be to make economic growth redundant. The catastrophic fall in the economy in the last two years, the amount of debt that has to paid off, and the need to provide for a rising population point to a necessity for modest and sustainable growth. What should be redundant, though, is growth *for its own sake*. By ceasing to measure everything by crude figures for GDP or GNP, we would be constantly forced to ask what kind of growth we were experiencing, whether it was helping to create a healthier and more secure society and whether it was capable of being sustained. If it's true that 'what we measure affects what we do', more realistic measuring should help to focus collective attention on what really needs to be done.

By adopting these new and more realistic ways of measuring progress, Ireland wouldn't just be sending out a signal to the rest of the world that it wants to be in the forefront of a larger change. It would also be sending out a signal to itself that the era of self-delusion is over.

PART TWO

Five Decencies

We have come to take it for granted that only very wealthy societies can guarantee a decent standard of well-being for all their citizens. In the 1990s even most of those on the left bought in to the belief that it was necessary to create enormous wealth – and therefore to have large numbers of super-rich individuals – in order to be able to redistribute some of it towards those in need. There is a logical sequence: generate the wealth and then divvy up some of it. Except that this sequence never turns out to be quite so logical – the right time to redistribute the wealth never arrives. However much money there is, we can't redistribute it because those who have it might take fright.

In fact, most of the real social prosperity of Western Europe was generated, not out of fabulous riches, but out of almost absolute poverty. The welfare states that made the 1950s and 1960s decades of tangible improvement in the lives and opportunities of the majority were built on foundations of rubble and despair. They didn't follow a period of unimpeded wealth creation. They followed a decade of woeful global depression and a savagely destructive world war that left most European cities in ruins. In London alone, three and a half million homes had been destroyed. There was just one intact bridge across the Rhine and not a single one across the Seine between Paris and the sea.

It is no harm, in our current state of gloom, to remind ourselves of what Europe looked like to a well-informed American traveller in 1947:

There is too little of everything – too few trains, trams,
buses and automobiles to transport people to work on
time, let alone take them on holidays; too little flour to
make bread without adulterants, and even so not enough
bread to provide energies for hard labour; too little paper
for newspapers to report more than a fraction of the
world's news; too little seed for planting and too little
fertilizer to nourish it; too few houses to live in and not
enough glass to supply them with window panes; too
little leather for shoes, wool for sweaters, gas for cook-
ing, cotton for diapers, sugar for jam, fats for frying, milk
for babies, soap for washing.

And yet, from this state, most European societies created,
within a decade, a framework of common decency – universal
health services and pensions, free primary and secondary education and in many cases free university enrolment, adequate
public housing and at least basic unemployment insurance.
Those systems, in turn, set in train the greatest era of general
rises in well-being that the continent has ever known.

What motivated this enormous effort? Fear, mostly. The
continent had experienced in the most vicious way the social
and political consequences of long-term economic depression.
It was almost impossible not to understand the ways in which
the erosion of living standards and the spread of deep anxiety
had unleashed a barbarism that had come close to destroying Europe. There was a new consensus that these conditions
could not be allowed to occur again. The way to prevent an-

other catastrophe was to organise society in such a way that everyone would have the right to the things that are necessary for people to live with dignity as full citizens of a democracy.

Tony Judt, in his classic *Postwar: A History of Europe since 1945*, asks and answers a fundamental question about the huge increase in resources going to public provision at a time of bleak general poverty: 'Why were Europeans willing to pay so much for [social] insurance and other long-term welfare provisions at a time when life was still truly hard and material shortages endemic? The first reason is that, precisely because times *were* difficult, the post-war welfare systems were a guarantee of a certain minimum of justice, or fairness.'

It would be absurd and obscene to compare Ireland's situation after the crash with that of Europe after Nazism, organised mass murder, catastrophic physical damage and a death toll of 36 million people – equivalent to the entire population of France at the start of the war. It is, however, worth noting that one of the things that defines Irish public culture is precisely the fact that it missed out, not just (most happily) on the war itself but (less happily) on this common European experience of rebuilding around a 'certain minimum of justice, or fairness'. That vast public enterprise of putting a floor of decency underneath the feet of every citizen is one we have never experienced.

Without in any way equating the depredations of Anglo Irish Bank with the existential horrors of the 1930s and 1940s, we can still see that some aspects of that era are present in very small ways in Ireland now. There is a profound loss of faith in democracy and traditional systems of authority. There is a significant degree of middle-class impoverishment. There is a rage fuelled by a deep sense of betrayal. And there is, above all, high anxiety. Fear is the keynote in Irish life –

fear of losing one's job or one's house or both; fear of being vulnerable and having to depend on public provision that is being stripped away by drastic cuts.

If there are some small-scale versions in Ireland of the great fear that corroded European democracy in the 1930s, there is also the possibility of learning from what Europeans eventually did to try to banish that fear. Having themselves learned in the hardest possible way, Europeans tried to inoculate themselves against the virus of mass fear with a system of basic guarantees to citizens. They gave themselves something to hold on to.

If Europeans could do that in the appalling circumstances of post-war trauma, Ireland can surely do so in the much more benign conditions in which it finds itself, even after the crash. To put it another way, Europe as a whole had to bring itself to the brink of annihilation before it understood what had to be done. Comparatively speaking, Ireland can learn the same lesson at a much lower cost. Mass unemployment, renewed emigration, negative equity and a decade of debt are a high enough price, but in the long view of history they are not high in the rank of horrors. The crisis may, in that same long view, be a price worth paying – *if* it forces us to construct a decent society.

The good news is that decency is perfectly possible. We have to ask what would constitute 'a guarantee of a certain minimum of justice, or fairness' for each citizen of the new republic. The answer, even in the twenty-first century, is not all that different from what it was in 1945. There are five things that a renewed Ireland is capable of providing for every citizen – security, health, education, equality and citizenship. If it does that, other less tangible benefits – pride, confidence, optimism, creativity – will follow.

Gimme Shelter:
The Decency of Security

If the great value of the last three decades has been the ac-
quisition of more stuff, the great value of the next three will
be security. There is, perhaps, a cycle in these things. The
generation that followed the terrible instabilities of the Great
Depression and the Second World War craved the comfort of
security. The next generation, whether it liked it or not, was
told to value risk, to kick away the certainties of the welfare
state and embrace the thrills and spills of a dynamic, ever-
changing world. 'Risk-taking', which had negative connotations for the older generation, was presented as an unquali-
fied virtue. It turned out, of course, that those who took the
real risks were not those who got the rewards. When the rich
gambled and won, they kept the proceeds. When they gambled and lost, society as a whole had to take the losses.

This is one of the reasons why the pendulum has swung
back again and the craving for security now trumps the supposed thrills of casino capitalism. The OECD has recently
reported, for example, that across OECD countries job security is now the attribute most valued by workers. In Ireland,
94 per cent of respondents cited job security as an important
job attribute, compared with 79 per cent who cited a high
income.

Risk-taking will always have its place in any dynamic

economy, but the consequences of unconfined gambling are now too evident and too painful. There are, besides, too many uncertainties and anxieties – technological change, seismic shifts in the global order, the existential threat of global warming, the impending exhaustion of the carbon economy – for humanity to live without some anchors in stability. No political system can turn the future into familiar territory. But a real republic can provide two tangible guarantees of security: a place to live and a dignified old age. By fixing housing and pensions, we can take some of the fear out of the future.

Pensions

If the sex lives of film stars are at one end of the spectrum of things that most people are curious about, pensions are at the other. Which is probably just as well. Pensions policy in Ireland is not a pretty sight. Put simply, we spend over €7 billion a year of public money in order to get one of the highest rates of pensioner poverty in the developed world. In the OECD as a whole, the average earner's pension replaces 60 per cent of his or her income. In Ireland, the figure is just 34 per cent. More than 30 per cent of Ireland's pensioners live in poverty. This is the third highest old-age poverty rate among the OECD countries and well over double the OECD average. Only Korea and Mexico of the thirty OECD countries have higher old-age poverty rates.

The good news is that this presents the opportunity to do something really significant. It is possible to redesign pensions in a way that guarantees every citizen at least a decent basic income in retirement. This would be, in twenty-first-century terms, the fulfilment of the promise made in the Democratic Programme of the First Dáil to create a republic which would take 'care of the Nation's aged and infirm, who shall not be regarded as a burden, but rather entitled to the Nation's gratitude and consideration'. It would also give those at work some sense of comforting certainty about the future. We just have to wean ourselves off the insane idea that the way to give people a secure old age is to get them to put their money into wildly insecure investments.

At the moment, pensions are being presented as a source, not of hope, but of fear. There is a rather crude attempt to panic people into accepting the erosion of both retirement age and pension benefits by talking of the 'demographic time bomb' of an ageing population. This notion needs to be examined calmly. Population projections are nearly always wrong. Even if we assume that the current ones (which show the number of people over sixty-five in Ireland increasing by 50 per cent in the next ten years and trebling by 2050) are correct, it does not follow that the idea of a civilised retirement has to be abandoned. In Ireland, if the projections are correct, public spending on pensions (both state pensions and public service pensions) will be 10.5 per cent of GDP in 2050. But in the eurozone as a whole, public spending on pensions is already 11 per cent of GDP. France and Germany have not yet fallen into the sea.

The demographics do need to be taken seriously, but what will really matter is the productivity, rather than the number, of those at work. (It is not that long ago, after all, that most women in the Western world were not in the paid workforce. This did not stop the development of universal pension systems in the 1950s.) It is also worth pointing out that Irish people already have unusually long working lives: the average exit age from the labour force is 64.1 in Ireland compared to the EU25 average of 61.2.

One use of the panic is to pave the way for the cutting of public retirement benefits. The other, however, is to stampede workers into private pension funds. Essentially, Irish policy is following the American model of encouraging workers to 'take responsibility' for their own retirement by investing their money in stock markets and property portfolios. Essentially, this move is from social security to personal insecurity.

The Irish private pensions industry is the worst in the developed world.[1] In the great financial crash of 2008, Irish pension funds managed to lose more than three times as much of their value as their counterparts in Germany. People would be better off putting their money in a post office savings account than investing it in a pension.

A post office savings certificate returns 21 per cent interest after five and a half years, with no fees and a state guarantee. Over the past three years, the average managed pension fund in Ireland has returned a stellar *minus* 7.6 per cent per annum. The five-year returns to the end of July 2010 were an average of *minus* 0.3 per cent per annum over this period. Irish group pension managed fund returns over the past ten years were 0.5 per cent a year on average, well below the Irish inflation rate of 2.5 per cent a year over the same period. Indeed, none of the managed funds outperformed inflation over this period, while four of the ten funds failed to deliver any gains at all – even before inflation is taken into account – over the last ten 10 years. The star performer, Eagle Star/Zurich Life, came in at 1.8 per cent annual return over the decade – 0.7 per cent worse than inflation. Allied Irish Bank Investment Managers achieved *minus* 0.7 per cent return – 3.2 per cent below inflation. The cream of the crop was KBC Asset Management, which earned a dazzling *minus* 1.7 per cent for its investors – 4.2 per cent below inflation.[2]

Even these dismal figures don't tell the full story. Out of the returns, the pension fund managers also take fees. No one actually knows for sure what the general level of fees in the Irish pensions industry is, but the best estimate is around 2.2 per cent per annum. This means that if a fund reports a return of 3 per cent, the real return for the investor is 0.8 per cent.

The performance of the state's National Pension Reserve Fund, into which 1 per cent of GNP (currently about €1.5 billion) is paid every year, is not much better. Since its inception in 2001, the fund has had a return on investment of just 1.7 per cent.[3] Over 30 per cent was wiped off its value in 2008. It has recovered significantly since then, but the overall return on investment is still no better than the rate of inflation.

This is where the fantasy starts. We know that over the last ten years private pension funds have earned virtually nothing for their investors. But we also know that the government, in its National Pensions Framework, is proposing to push all workers into private pension schemes in which they will automatically be enrolled. (They can opt out, but otherwise will be assumed to have opted in.)

What rate of return will these schemes deliver? You have to look very hard in the National Pensions Framework to find the answer in a footnote, where it lists the 'reasonable assumptions over a 40 year period' that underlie the strategy. One of the key assumptions is '7 per cent investment returns'. In other words, privately managed funds that have delivered 0.5 per cent return a year, over the last ten years, will somehow produce fourteen times that return – 7 per cent a year – over the next forty years. Samuel Johnson called a second marriage 'the triumph of hope over experience'. When it comes to pensions, the government is Elizabeth Taylor.

The pensions economist Jim Stewart sums up the prospects of this scheme nicely: 'It is most unlikely that this scheme will succeed in providing adequate retirement income. The contribution periods will not be as forecast, given periods of unemployment, working abroad, or caring for children and other family members. Returns will certainly not be as forecast.'[4]

What's at stake here is public, as well as private, money. The state spends a lot of money on pensions – nearly €9 billion a year if we include the money going into the National Pension Reserve Fund. But the breakdown of this figure is where things get interesting – in three ways. Firstly, just €4.3 billion goes to paying the state pension to retired citizens. Another €3 billion goes on tax reliefs for the accumulation of private pensions. Of this €3 billion, 80 per cent goes to the top 20 per cent of earners.[5] It is a subsidy to those who least need subsidies.

Secondly, this spending is extremely high by international standards. Tax breaks for pensions account for 2.2 per cent of net national income in Ireland, compared to 0.2 per cent in Finland, 0.8 per cent in Norway, 0.4 per cent in Spain and one per cent in the USA.[6]

Thirdly, this state expenditure on private pensions is strikingly ineffective. It does not do what it is supposed to – give workers in general the security of knowing that they will not have a massive drop in their incomes when they retire. This very expensive policy has failed. Just 54 per cent of employees have a pension fund. Just 37 per cent of employees under thirty have a pension – a serious problem, given that an early start is the key to a decent income in retirement. In low-paid sectors of the economy, pension coverage is disastrously thin: 77 per cent of hotel and restaurant workers and 64 per cent of retail trade workers have no pension.[7] There is a stark gender gap: among employees, 56 per cent of men but just 50 per cent of women have a pension. But because so many older women were never in the paid workforce, it is estimated that three out of every four Irish women rely solely on the state pension.

The last big effort to get ordinary employees to invest in private pension funds – Personal Retirement Savings Accounts (PRSAs) – was a disaster. Gerard Hughes and Jim Stewart, in their book *Personal Provision of Retirement Income* (2010), point out that 'there are just about 6 per cent of firms in which employees have availed of the opportunity to contribute to a PRSA. The average number of contributors per firm is just three and a half.' Even these figures mask the full extent of the problem – the average contributor to a PRSA is paying far too little to ensure an adequate income in retirement.

Though no one talks about it very much, there is a huge crisis in private pension schemes. Three out of four private sector company schemes are in deficit and, according to the Pensions Board in its latest annual report, the combined shortfall now amounts to €25 billion. The schemes of many public sector companies are also in a terrible state: the ESB's pension fund is €2 billion short of its projected liabilities; CIE has a deficit of over €500 million; Bord na Mona's is €20 million short.

Moreover, Irish pension funds have learned nothing from the disaster they inflicted on their members by engaging in risky investments in property and the stock market at the height of the boom. The most recent report of the Pensions

Board reveals that the funds that lost money in the crash because they had put their client's money into risky ventures are now trying to make up those losses – by putting their client's money into risky ventures:

> Since investment losses emerged in 2007, there has been much talk about reducing pension risk and a number of schemes have taken specific action. However, all available data shows that there is as yet no significant change in the aggregate investment allocation of Irish defined benefit schemes. In 2007, Board data showed no demonstrable relationship between defined benefit scheme liabilities and investments, despite trustee obligations under the [law] . . . Our investigations in 2009 show very little change. The situation for defined contribution schemes is worryingly similar: there is very little risk reduction in the funds in which many members are invested. It is difficult to avoid the conclusion that the good 2009 investment returns are a result of the same strategies that caused much of the recent losses, and that the chances of further losses are therefore too high.[8]

In other words, the private pension funds are like addictive gamblers. They played for high stakes and suffered catastrophic losses. They went back to the table and their number came up. Now they think they're back in the game and they're putting all their clients' chips on the roulette wheel again. There is just one intelligent conclusion to be drawn from this behaviour: if they haven't learned from the implosion of the markets in 2007 and 2008, they will never learn. And if the government pushes more punters into their arms with the promise of a 7 per cent annual return over forty years, it will be feeding a steady supply of hallucinogens to an industry addicted to risk.

But these risks are increasingly being forced onto ordinary workers. There has been a large shift from defined benefit schemes (of which there are 1,200 in Ireland) to much riskier defined contribution schemes (of which there are 83,000). The difference is neatly summed up by Teresa Ghilarducci: 'In defined benefit plans, employers make all the investment decisions and must pay the pension regardless of the pension fund's investment earnings. In a defined contribution plan, the employee makes all the decisions and accepts the risk that the accumulation in her account could be lower than expected.'[9]

Even for the better-off half of the population within the system of private occupational pensions, the benefits are heavily skewed towards those at the top. Professor Gerry Hughes of the TCD business school studied the annual accounts of 45 large Irish companies. He found that the average annual pension contribution made by the company for an executive director was €124,000, compared with around €2,700 for other covered employees. Almost 40 per cent of executive directors benefited from contributions of €50,000 or more while a quarter of them benefited from contributions of €100,000 or more. Pension contributions made by the companies for their executive directors – all of them subsidised by the taxpayer – were 31 per cent of their salaries. Those for ordinary employees were 8.5 per cent.[10] Hughes reckoned that 'some executive directors need only to work for half of the time other employees have to work to qualify for a full pension, that the normal retirement age may be three to five years lower than for other employees, that if the average executive director were to take immediate retirement,

he would have a pension 15 times greater than the income
of the average single pensioner and that the average value of
an executive director's pension fund amounts to nearly €4.7
million, compared with €102,000 for other employees'. (An
individual can accumulate a pension pot of €5.4 million before tax kicks in.)

Or, to put it more bluntly, the system is heavily rigged in
favour of the wealthiest. The summit of this grotesque fix
was scaled by Michael Fingleton, chief executive of Irish
Nationwide Building Society. His stewardship left the taxpayer with a bill for €5.4 billion in bad debts. He retired
with a pension pot of €27.6 million so that he could enjoy
his old age in satisfied reflection on his incomparable contribution to Irish society.

The same pattern holds with public sector pensions, which
are generally thought to be lavish. At the top, they are not so
much lavish as opulent. The director of the employment and
training agency Fas, Rody Molloy, received a lump sum of
€450,000 and an annual pension of €111,000 when he was
forced to resign after revelations of extraordinary behaviour
in the agency.[11] Patrick Neary, the Financial Regulator who
struck such fear into the Irish banks that they wet themselves
laughing, was eased out with a pension of €140,000 a year.
The new chief executive of the HSE, Cathal Magee, will get
a contribution to his private pension fund of a quarter of his
basic salary – in other words, €80,500 a year into his pension pot. But for most public servants, pensions are decidedly
modest. In the health sector, for example, pensions average a
modest €14,800 a year. Given that this includes some people
– hospital consultants or senior HSE managers – who have
huge pensions, the pension for the ordinary nurse or hospital
porter is surely much lower.

The people who benefit so lavishly from this system will fight like pit bull terriers to preserve the current pensions policy, as will the pensions industry, whose dismal performance is clouded by the generous tax breaks. (Without the tax benefits, no rational person would favour a managed pension over the post office or even the mattress.) But the benefits of breaking this system are immense. Even in tough times, Ireland can guarantee every citizen a modest but decent income in retirement – *if* it stops believing in the fantasy that private pension funds, which have learned nothing from the bursting of the boomtime bubble, will magically produce an unbroken sequence of solid returns on investment over the next forty years.

The core of the answer to the pensions problem is so obvious it is almost invisible: the state old-age pension. The state pension has actually been a very effective way of lifting older people out of poverty. Because of modest but steady increases in the rates between 2004 and 2008, consistent poverty for older people has fallen from 3.9 per cent to 1.4 per cent, while the proportion of older people at risk of poverty has fallen from 27 per cent to just over 11 per cent. There is no evidence, on the other hand, that private pensions have done anything to lift older people out of poverty – given their dismal rate of return, it is not clear that they have actually increased the overall sum of money available to support people in retirement. Retired people in Ireland get the vast bulk of their income from the state pension – 69 per cent of median income for those aged sixty-four to seventy-five and 87 per cent for those aged over seventy-five.

From the €9 billion the state currently spends on public and private pensions every year, it can well afford a very significant increase in the old-age pension. The Tasc/TCD Pensions

Policy Group proposals are the only ones that remove dependency on risky market investments, end the massive bias towards the better-off and guarantee everyone a decent basic income in retirement.

The stages in this process are:

Increase the state old-age pension from its current level of 32 per cent of average earnings to at least 40 per cent. Make this pension universal – available to everyone regardless of their previous status. This will cost less than half the current cost of tax reliefs on private pension contributions.

Establish a new Social Insurance Retirement Fund. This will be mandatory for all workers, employed and self-employed. It will be a defined benefit scheme and will guarantee all workers, in tandem with the increased state pension, at least 50 per cent of their salary in retirement, up to a specified maximum. It will be funded by earnings-related *equal* contributions paid by the employee, the employer and the state. While the Social Insurance pension will primarily be related to income, contribution credits will be awarded for periods spent on family duties (such as childcare and eldercare) or in further education, and will also be paid during periods of unemployment or disability. This would be particularly, but not exclusively, beneficial to women.

Standard-rate all pension-related tax reliefs at 20 per cent, and reduce to €75,000 the ceiling on earnings which may be taken into account for tax relief purposes.

I would add a further proposal: stop paying the €1.5 billion or so a year that the state is currently putting into the National Pension Reserve Fund. At the moment, the state is borrowing this money at high interest rates in order to put it into a fund which invests it on international stock markets. If any of us knew a friend who was borrowing money and going to the bookies to put it on the horses, we would know that intervention was called for. It would make far more sense to use this money to increase the old-age pension.

This new system has the considerable advantage of ending the current divisions between public and private sector workers. Everyone will have the same basic benefits and make proportionally the same contribution to the social insurance top-up element of the pension.

Housing

If the free market could meet the basic human need for adequate shelter in decent communities, Ireland would have the best-housed population in the world. Almost 800,000 new houses or apartments were built between January 1996 and December 2009 – one for every 5.6 people in Ireland. In the last years of the boom, there was a tumult of house-building that is, in relative terms, unparalleled in human history. It was like a crack epidemic in Legoland. Even when there were too many houses, the building continued. Two figures say it all: a quarter of a million houses empty in 2006 and a quarter of a million more houses built between 2006 and 2010.

This mania of construction could have been a controlled experiment in what happens when a house ceases to be a home and becomes a commodity. When the music stopped, two large groups of citizens were left out in the cold. Very large numbers of people had paid far, far too much for their houses: at the beginning of September 2010 one in twenty mortgages (over 36,000 in all) were in arrears for more than 90 days and around half of all mortgage holders (some 200,000 home-owners) were heading for negative equity. But there was also another group that had lost out: those for whom the market had no use in the first place.

The number of people who were officially homeless doubled during the boom years, from 2,500 in 1996 to over 5,000 in 2008.[12] But this was only the most extreme manifestation of a much larger social problem. In 2005 economists P. J. Drudy and Michael Punch estimated what they considered to be the real number of those in 'housing need' – unable to afford a home, living in low-standard accommodation (there are, for example, 8,750 bedsits in the country, housing 14,500 people),[13] receiving rent supplement payments from the state and/or on local authority waiting lists for social housing. They reckoned that 105,900 households, or 250,000 people, were in real housing need.[14] This number is likely to have increased sharply after 2005 as the cost of buying or renting houses continued to soar. People earning below the average industrial wage never made up a large slice of the mortgage market, but that slice was actually getting smaller during the manic phase of the boom. Those with a combined income of €30,000 or less accounted for 4 per cent of new mortgages in 2000, but less than 1 per cent in 2006.

If we put these two categories together – those currently unable to pay their high mortgages and those who never got adequate housing in the first place – the housing boom has left around 200,000 families in a very bad way. Even leaving aside the long-term effects of unemployment and economic depression and thinking only about the immediate effects in terms of housing, far too many people were left without the security of a decent home they can comfortably call their own.

This – as well as the wider banking and economic crises that are rooted in the property boom – is the result of a con-

scious, ideologically driven, political choice. The Fianna Fáil/
Progressive Democrats governments of 1997 onwards decided to abandon the idea of housing as first and foremost a
social need. They defined it instead as a market commodity.
The job of the state was not to assist citizens to form decent
communities, but to stimulate that market which would, in
turn, do what markets inevitably do – produce the best possible outcomes for everyone. Thus a range of measures – the
abandonment of residential property taxes, increased mortgage interest relief, a reduction in capital gains tax from 40
per cent to 20 per cent, tax reliefs for property development
and investment (including Section 23 relief, urban renewal
schemes, town renewal schemes, rural renewal schemes and
the seaside resort schemes) – was used to 'stimulate' a housing market that was actually in as much need of stimulus as a
hyped-up four year-old who has discovered the mother lode
of Coco Pops.

In the ultimate triumph of the idea of the house as a commodity, by 2007, Bank of Ireland was lending as much
money to buy-to-let and speculative 'flippers', as to first-time
buyers and over a quarter of all new homes that year were
bought by speculators. The revenue foregone on the range of
property-related tax shelters – €1.9 billion – would have built
6,400 social houses at an average cost of €300,000 each.

While the private sector was having its fancy tickled at
every turn, the public sector – both local authority and voluntary housing – was being subjected to sensory deprivation.
This was not primarily about money. Ireland managed significant social housing development even in the lean years
of the 1930s, 1940s and 1950s. In the 1930s local authority
housing represented 60 per cent of all new homes; the proportion rose as high as 70 per cent in the mid-1940s, and was

always above 50 per cent of total housing output in the early to mid-1950s. During the boom years of 1995 to 2007, local authority housing averaged just 6 per cent of total output, fewer than 3,500 houses a year. But because local authorities continued to sell off houses, the net gain to local authority housing stock over this period was a mere 1,790 houses a year. Houses built by voluntary associations, meanwhile, made up just 2 per cent of completions – 1,139 a year on average. In other words, fewer than 3,000 social or voluntary homes were being added every year during a craze that reached its peak at close to 90,000 houses a year.

This disparity was all about power – those who had it and those who did not. People who could not afford to do their bit in blowing up the property bubble didn't count at all. The construction industry and those in banking, land speculation and property development who had a stake in it hardly stopped counting – up to several billion.

This imbalance of power was crystallised in a single reversal of government policy. In 2002, at a time when concern about the unaffordability of housing was not yet drowned out by the fairground barkers of the property industry, the Fianna Fáil/ PD government introduced what was called Part V of the Planning Act. It allowed local authorities to impose as a condition for the granting of planning permission for new housing developments, a requirement that 20 per cent of the land be transferred to be used for social and affordable housing. Alternatively, developers could transfer finished houses or prepared sites. It looked for a moment as if Fianna Fáil and their sidekicks had, for once, actually faced down the developers and put the overall public interest first. (It is worth noting – because alleged constitutional difficulties are always cited by those opposed to any controls on private developers – that Part V was upheld by the Supreme Court as complying with the constitutional balance between private property and the common good.)

The moment was brief – two years, to be precise. The property industry hated Part V – not just because it imposed social obligations on them but also because it suggested that there ought to be at least some degree of social mingling in new housing developments, with those who were less well off living alongside those who could afford (or rather, be allowed to pretend that they could afford) mortgages. The Confederation of Irish Industry and the Irish Home Builders Association lobbied hard to have Part V defanged. And, of course, they got what they wanted. The same government that had introduced Part V in 2000 abandoned it in 2002. An amendment to the Planning Act allowed developers to provide cash instead of homes or, crucially, to provide the social houses somewhere else, so that they would not contaminate the purity of their new estates.

The attitudes underlying this opposition were revealed in a surprisingly candid speech by Alan Cooke of the Irish Auctioneers & Valuers Institute. Speaking in October 1999, when the original Part V was due to come into force, he lamented the lost golden age of segregation: 'In future, people will speak of pre- and post-1999 developments . . . whether they live in mixed developments or are among the lucky few residing in segregated private schemes. Of course, we don't approve of such snobbish attitudes – publicly. Privately, however, most of us will continue to do what we have always done – pay considerably more to be among the latter group.'[15] Happily for the republic, the principle of social segregation was restored by the industry's remarkable powers of persuasion.

At the same time, the belief that the private sector would solve the problems of run-down working-class estates proved illusory. Some of the worst concentrations of poor housing and social deprivation were to be transformed by giving property developers generous deals under public/private partnership (PPP) arrangements. There was one significant success (Fatima Mansions in Dublin), but for the most part the PPP model achieved nothing beyond the anguish of false promises. In Dublin, five PPPs involving the tycoon Bernard McNamara collapsed: O'Devaney Gardens, Dominick Street, St Michael's Estate, Infirmary Road and Sean McDermott Street. In Limerick the plan to regenerate some of the most deprived and alienated areas of the country hinged on the notion of selling private houses to fund the social housing. Private developers were to invest €1.3 billion of the €3 billion cost of regeneration. By the beginning of 2010, it was clear that this simply wasn't going to happen.

The catastrophic failure of this whole approach to housing leaves two huge and interrelated tasks: to clean up the mess and to establish radically different priorities for the future.

The first task is formidably difficult, will take many years, and has been made much harder by the government's strategy of rescuing banks rather than mortgage holders and of gambling, through Nama, on a re-inflation of the property market. If these strategies have advanced to a point of no return, room to manoeuvre will be extremely limited.

The place to start, however, is with a recognition of brutal reality: the building boom is not coming back. Blithe optimism about an 'upturn in the market' is plainly idiotic. In May 2010, 112,506 new or second-hand housing units were for sale in Ireland, with another 20,463 available for rent. There are currently 350,000 empty houses (including holiday homes) and an oversupply in the market of somewhere between 120,000 and 170,000 houses and apartments. That's about three and a half years' worth of new housing demand, even assuming that the number of new households continues to rise at boomtime levels, which it won't. Some counties, like Leitrim and Longford, have enough empty houses to last them for at least the next ten years.

The same is true of the amount of land zoned by local authorities: South Dublin has twenty years of zoned development land on its books; Dublin City has thirty-five years; Cork City has fifty years. Who says the Irish authorities don't think ahead? And the commercial market is also suffering the consequences of hyper-development. In 1990 there were a million square metres of office space in Dublin; in the middle of 2010 there were 750,000 square metres of *empty* office space in Dublin.

According to the National Institute for Regional and Spatial Analysis, 'there is little need for housing development in the state in the immediate future beyond selected social housing provision'.[16] The obvious corollary is that at least we know where the solutions do not lie – in any broad attempts to stimulate the property market.

The second thing that has to be recognised is that, while it would be delightful if all the people in housing need could be housed in the vacant properties left behind by the boom, this can't happen. There are nearly 20,000 houses or apartments in 620 ghost estates. But many of these estates were left in a poor state and many are already falling into complete dilapidation. And many are in parts of the country where the demand for social housing is relatively limited. There is no point in moving homeless or poorly housed people from Dublin and Cork to Leitrim and Longford, without public transport, family networks, services or employment prospects. There certainly should be a rigorous analysis (independent of Nama) of all the housing that the state has ended up owning by default to see which properties are genuinely suitable for social housing. These properties should be handed over to voluntary housing associations as quickly as possible, so that potentially decent housing is not lost through dilapidation. But turning ghost estates into ghettoes will simply add yet another toxic element to the legacy of the boom.

Even if some social housing can be salvaged from Nama, there is still a need for a long-term plan to ensure that everyone has access to shelter at an affordable price and in a sustainable community. This would require a complete reversal of current government policy, which is to slash the budget for social housing. In the review of the National Development Plan unveiled in July 2010, the budget for social housing was slashed from €17 billion over seven years to just €4.4 billion – a cut far greater than the fall in the cost of building houses. The implication is that everything will somehow return to the way it was before the crash and the market will do what it so obviously failed to do during the boom years – guarantee decent housing for everyone.

Fulfilling that guarantee is perfectly feasible within current resources. But three conditions have to be fulfilled first.

The first of these is that the state stops wasting money on the cost of keeping poorer people in substandard accommodation.

The state is by far the largest customer of private landlords in Ireland. An extraordinary 50 per cent of all tenants in the private rented sector are in receipt of the social welfare rent supplement, up from 41 per cent in 2007.[17] This is what happens when you neglect social housing – poorer people end up renting flats and apartments and the state ends up paying much of the cost to the landlords. What does the state – and more importantly the tenants – get in return?

The 2006 census showed that average rents in the private sector were €828 a month, compared to €255 in local authority housing. This was not because the private apartments were all palatial. On the contrary, in Dublin City 40 per cent of private rental dwellings inspected by the local authority in 2006 and 42 per cent inspected in 2007 did not meet minimum standards. In Cork City 45 per cent inspected in 2006 and 36 per cent inspected in 2007 were sub-standard. These figures did not improve significantly with the bursting of the property bubble. In 2009 42 per cent of rented accommodation in Dublin city, and a third in Cork and Limerick cities, was substandard.

Yet the cost of paying for this substandard accommodation has been horrendous. This is partly because the numbers of people needing help to pay their rent increased rapidly in the boom years – from 36,800 in 1997 to a high of 60,179 in 2005. But it is also because landlords were able to ride the wave of rising property values and screw the state for ever higher rents. While the number of recipients of rent supplements rose by 64 per cent, the cost of the payments rose by almost 400 per cent. In 2009 the state spent almost half a billion euro on rent supplements.

Equally wasteful are the other, haphazard state schemes for emergency shelter. Focus Ireland pointed out that it costs €30,000 a year to keep a single person in emergency accommodation – usually supplied in the totally unsuitable environment of B&Bs. It costs €80,000 to keep a young person in residential state care and €91,000 to keep someone in prison. By contrast, Focus Ireland's own proposals for decent,

suitable, supported housing for vulnerable people were cost-
ed at €12,000 a year for high-support accommodation (with
24-hour supervision); €6,000 a year for medium-support
schemes; and €4,800 for low-support accommodation.[18] As
well as all the social and personal benefits that accrue, acting
decently would also be cheaper.

Instead of pouring money into the bank accounts of private landlords in return for what are at best inadequate and
short-term answers to the need for a home, the state should
be putting the money into the creation of decent communities. To take the €500 million spent on rent allowances as a
case in point: €500 million over twenty years is €10 billion,
enough to build 50,000 houses at a cost of €200,000 a unit.

As well as this €500 million, there is another €877 million
which can and should be redirected from current expenditure
towards social housing. This is the sum spent on tax breaks
for landlords in 2007.[19] The tax break means that landlords
can set against their rental income the cost of the money they
borrowed to buy the property they are renting out. This is
a completely pointless incentive for buy-to-let owners. Put
together with the spending on rent supplement, it represents
an annual transfer to landlords from the state of €1.3 billion
– complete insanity in a country that is pockmarked with
surplus properties. This money should be going to social
housing instead.

A full-scale commitment to social housing would undoubtedly cost more than this, and there is a need for investment
up-front before the savings on rent allowances and other subsidies to private rental can kick in. (It would obviously take
time for those who currently depend on rent subsidies to be
moved into social housing.) Some saving can be made by giving voluntary housing associations, which have an excellent

track record in building and managing housing schemes, to take a leading role. The associations can combine public with private funding to multiply the effect of state investment.

It would also make sense to shift some of the currently planned infrastructural spending away from trophy projects like the Dublin Metro (hardly an urgent priority in the midst of a social and fiscal emergency). A focused and innovative programme of well-planned social housing would have far more immediate impact on well-being in Ireland than almost any of the planned infrastructural projects.

The cost of a serious commitment to social housing can be contained, however, if the second condition is fulfilled. This is that we bring down the cost of building land. At the heart of the property mania of the boom years was a huge transfer of wealth from those buying houses to landowners. To put this transfer into perspective, even at a relatively early stage of the boom, for counties Meath and Kildare in the Dublin commuter belt alone, it was, at €7 billion, greater than the state's annual expenditure on health.[20] The primary reason why houses were so over-valued is because the cost of the land became an ever larger proportion of the overall cost of a house. Eithne Fitzgerald and Nessa Winston calculated that between 1995 and 2002 alone, the cost of the site went from 21 per cent of the price of the house to 53 per cent. This created the biggest bonanza of unearned wealth in Ireland since the huge land seizures that followed the Cromwellian conquest.

This massive enrichment of a small minority was actually enhanced by government policy. In 1998, when landowners were apparently hoarding their acres, the Bacon report recommended a carrot-and-stick scheme – a reduction of capital gains tax on development land to 20 per cent for four years, followed by an increase to 60 per cent. Anyone tuned in to the Fianna Fáil system can guess what happened next. The government dropped the tax to 20 per cent and then somehow forgot to put it up to 60 per cent after four years.

This habit of enriching a minority at the expense of the ability of everyone else to have access to a decent home has to be broken. As already argued, the Kenny Report of 1974, which recommended that local authorities be enabled to acquire building land at the existing agricultural value plus 25 per cent, must be implemented. Why, indeed, has the government not done so already, in the wake of the crash?

The reason is simple enough: it does not want to face up to a hard decision – to make relatively cheap housing a fixed central aim of public policy. This may seem like an obvious statement of intent, but it is genuinely tough. The country still has a huge amount invested – both literally and in psychological terms – in the notion that house prices are going to rise significantly. Nama is based on this belief. People in negative equity are banking on it. But we have to face the fact that house prices above the Western European average are socially destructive and economically disastrous. They turn housing into a commodity rather than a right. They divert investment into unproductive assets. They drive up costs in the rest of the economy, damaging the competitiveness of Irish businesses. They feed into general construction and rental costs for companies seeking to invest in Ireland – in 2009, in spite of the crash, Ireland was the third most expensive country in Europe in which both to build a prime industrial site and to rent such a site.

Framing rises in the property market as 'good news' is delusional. Governments need to have the guts to articulate this truth and to set down as a long-term national policy that house prices will be kept in line with those in other Western European countries.

To make such a policy real, Kenny has to be implemented. The new local governments should have extensive powers to decide on appropriate land-use policies, within the framework of a clear national spatial strategy. It is striking, for example, that what is now the National Transportation Authority was meant to be the Dublin Land Use and Transportation Authority. The dropping of any reference to 'land use' in official policy was one of the fatal signals for the property frenzy to take off. Conversely, the adoption of land-use strategies at local, regional and national level, with proper powers of enforcement, could signal the beginning of a new approach to development.

The third vital condition for guaranteeing decent housing for everyone is a shift in cultural attitudes. Attitudes have to change in two respects – rental and segregation.

In Ireland, with half of all private rentals taken up by people in receipt of social welfare, renting is generally a mark either of youth or of poverty. The craving for 'home' that is deeply rooted in Irish culture – shaped by histories of both dispossession and displacement – manifests itself in the feeling that long-term renting is for losers. Buying a house is not so much an option as a necessity. And this is a self-fulfilling prophecy – the scarcity in the rental market of prosperous, long-term clients has led to a weak regime of protection for tenants. Most EU countries, for example, have regimes in which tenants can get relatively long leases with rent increases linked to the consumer price index. Ireland does not. Even basic rights for tenants cannot be taken for granted. Landlords routinely refuse to return deposits. Rent books are not kept. Illegal evictions are commonplace.

It is easy to forget in this Irish context that home ownership is not the norm in most Western European countries,
including some of the most prosperous ones. In Ireland home
ownership is around 77 per cent. In Germany it is 43 per cent,
in Sweden 38 per cent, and in Switzerland 37 per cent.[20] Getting over the obsession with owning one's own home and
encouraging more secure long-term rental would do a lot
to bring sanity to the overall housing market. It would also
mean an end to what has become an almost automatic right
of long-term social housing tenants to buy their homes.

We also need to get over our snobbery about social housing. In Ireland, social and voluntary housing are, like rental,
heavily associated with poverty. The result has been a dangerous social segregation, with mortgage-holders geographi-
cally separated from the rest. Again, it is worth remembering
that this is not necessarily the norm in Western Europe. In
Sweden, Denmark and the Netherlands social housing makes
up 24, 27 and 35 per cent respectively of all homes. In Am-
sterdam social housing actually dominates the market, with
fourteen voluntary housing associations owning 55 per cent
of the stock.

It is possible to have an Ireland with more integrated and
sustainable communities in which housing is treated as one
of the basic entitlements of citizenship. Such a place would
look a lot more like a republic. It would also look more like
home.

2

Beyond the Sickness System:
The Decency of Health

Ask most people in Ireland about spending on health, and they will probably tell you that Ireland spends much less than most European countries. The assumption is not unreasonable – after all, most other countries seem to have much better health systems in which people can do extraordinary things like walk into a hospital and get treatment. It is, however, wrong. If you put together public and private spending on healthcare in Ireland, we spend in the region of $3,800 per person a year on health services. This is more than in Germany, France, Belgium, Sweden, Denmark, the UK, Australia, Spain or Japan.[1]

Health spending now accounts for almost 10 per cent of GNP – almost the same as in countries like Norway, Sweden, Britain and the Netherlands, all of which have universal healthcare systems of a much higher standard. Moreover, Ireland has a relatively young population – there are just 63,000 people over eighty-five – and therefore somewhat less demand on its health services. The percentage of the population reporting 'good' or 'very good' health in Ireland is higher than in any other country in the EU.[2] This ought to mean our euros go further in the healthcare system. In fact, we get a service that is patchy, hard to access, highly inequitable and sometimes downright squalid.

If we were designing a health system in a vacuum, it would make sense to build a proper national health service, funded by a fair taxation system. In practice, though, this would be enormously difficult in a society where half the population has private health insurance, GPs work as independent businesses, and the hospital system has evolved with an almost random mix of state- and Church-run, public, private, for-profit and not-for-profit institutions.

The Irish system is a mass of contradictions. In theory, everyone is entitled to free public hospital care, but official Department of Health policy is 'to encourage people to take responsibility for their own health and for their own health-care costs where this is possible'.[3] In this context 'take responsibility for' means 'pay for'.

Fifty per cent of people have private health insurance, but it contributes only about 10 per cent of the total cost of health care in Ireland. (Seventy-five per cent comes from taxation and 15 per cent from out-of-pocket payments such as GP fees and charges for A&E.) That 10 per cent, however, skews the entire system, creating a two-tier health system that is the antithesis of what a republic ought to be about.

This system achieves the triple whammy of being grossly unfair, grossly inefficient and grossly ineffective. It is unfair because it enforces a system of health apartheid, giving those who can afford private insurance access to treatment more quickly than those who cannot. It is inefficient because it is hopelessly complicated, requires a gigantic bureaucracy to run it and because it pulls off the breathtaking trick of creating incentives for hospitals and doctors *not* to treat patients. And it is ineffective because it discourages people from using the simplest ways of staying healthy and pays almost no attention to the idea of keeping people well. It is not a health system – it is a sickness system. Let's consider each of these achievements in a little more detail, in order to grasp the need for radical change.

Unfair:

As an official Department of Health report put it in July 2010, 'individuals who can afford private health insurance gain access to some hospital services faster than those with equivalent health needs but who do not have insurance'. Or, to put it another way, the lives of citizens with money are worth more than those of citizens without money. It would be hard to think of any better way of summarising what it means *not* to live in a republic.

In August 2010, for example, 1,073 public patients were waiting more than three months for a colonoscopy – a test that is of crucial importance in the early diagnosis of bowel cancer, a disease that kills around a thousand Irish people every year. For those with private health insurance, colonoscopies are available almost immediately in urgent cases or within a few weeks for routine tests.

The two-tier health system creates and sustains bad health. As the Health Service Executive acknowledges, 'In Ireland, there is a clear social gradient where health status continuously improves as one moves up the social class ladder, and declines as one moves down it. Morbidity and mortality are higher in the lower social class groups than in the higher groups.' In the EU *Survey on Income and Living Conditions in Ireland*, 85 per cent of those who were 'non-poor' reported good or very good health, whereas this was true of only 66 per cent of those experiencing income poverty. Eleven per cent of men with the highest 10 per cent of incomes had a chronic illness. This rose to 20 per cent for those in the middle of the income range, and to 42 per cent for those in the second lowest decile.

On the island of Ireland, the death rate for almost every cause is 100 to 200 per cent higher in the lowest occupational class than the rate in the highest occupational class.[4] It has been estimated that 5,400 fewer people would die prematurely each year across the island of Ireland if social deprivation and inequalities were tackled.

(There is, happily, an Irish solution to the Irish problem of health inequalities. It is no longer possible for researchers to correlate health outcomes for those under eighteen with social class. Class is measured by one classification system and health status by another. The problem will gradually disappear because nobody will be able to measure it.)[5]

Inefficient:

There is a common assumption that moving towards greater equality would mean sacrificing the efficiency of the market. In fact, inequity is also grossly inefficient. The high cost of GP visits stops people making regular visits to their doctor. The result is that serious medical conditions (high blood pressure, cancers, heart complaints) get diagnosed later, are harder to treat and cost the system more money.

The expert group on health funding sketches the following scenario, which arises from the fact that patients with health insurance can have antibiotic treatments administered at home, while those without insurance can't:

> Two patients are sitting on chairs in an overcrowded
> Accident and Emergency (A&E) department in Dublin
> with exactly the same clinical condition (cellulitis). Once
> diagnosed, Patricia, the patient with VHI insurance, goes

home to her own bed with a nurse visiting three times a
day to administer antibiotics. Pauline, the public patient,
has to wait in A&E to be attended and then admitted.
Although only requiring 'hotel' facilities and regular in-
travenous injections, her insurance status means that she
will occupy a very scarce hospital bed for about five days.

Recent research indicates that in the European Union as
a whole inequality-related health losses amount to more
than 700,000 deaths per year, the loss of 11.4 million life
years, and 33 million cases of ill health. The authors estimate
that these losses account for 20 per cent of the total costs of
healthcare and 15 per cent of the total costs of social security
benefits.[6] On this basis, it is possible to make an admittedly
crude calculation of the cost of health inequalities in Ireland,
given that the health budget is €15 billion and the social
welfare budget is roughly €20 billion. The cost of health inequalities in Ireland is €6 billion a year.

Aside from the inefficiencies rooted in inequality, however,
there are those rooted in craziness. The HSE is the largest
employer in the State (and also the largest purchaser in the
State, spending €4 billion a year on goods and services). The
number of whole-time equivalent staff rose by 39 per cent
between 2000 and 2007. It currently employs 111,000 people. Of these, 16 per cent are managers or administrators.
That's nearly 18,000 administrators.

Good managers are as important in the delivery of healthcare as good nurses or doctors, but the creation of the HSE
as a top-heavy bureaucracy is one of the great follies of the
age. It has ten 'national directors'. Its human resources division has a head of employee relations, a head of performance management and management information, a head of

recruitment and employer branding, a head of succession management, a head of leadership development, a head of change and processes, and a head of shared services. But it also has four regional HR directors, who presumably actually direct human resources. Equally, the HSE doesn't have a press officer. It has a national director of communications, a head of national press and media relations, a head of internal communications, a head of public communications and four area communications managers. And it is still perhaps the hardest organisation in Ireland to get information out of.

Such people don't come cheap. When a new chief executive, Cathal Magee, was being appointed in 2010, it turned out that he couldn't possibly work for the official salary of €228,000 but would generously settle for €350,000 plus a car allowance of €20,000.[7] (The chief executive of the NHS in the UK, a vastly larger organisation, is paid around €312,000.) The director of the cancer control programme is paid €237,000. The other national directors are officially paid between €140,000 and €170,000, though some are paid more based on personal contracts.

Yet it is hard to begrudge them the money, because the system they run is enough to drive anyone to despair. If the British health system was created by Nye Bevan, the Irish health system was created by Heath Robinson. Not even the greatest managerial genius could run this system well.

There are five different kinds of hospital: public hospitals owned by the state; 'voluntary' (usually Church-run) hospitals that operate within the public system; private not-for-profit hospitals (usually run by groups of medical consultants in conjunction with religious orders), often located alongside a public hospital and sharing some of its senior medical staff; free-standing private for-profit hospitals, often run by multinational healthcare businesses; and private for-profit hospitals co-located with a public hospital. And there are actually – in terms of their entitlements – four different kinds of patients: 'medical card' holders, who are entitled (in theory at least) to fully free services from GPs and in public hospitals; 'dual cover' patients who have both a medical card and private health insurance; 'non-covered' patients who have neither a medical card nor private health insurance; and patients with private health insurance only. Almost all doctors end up getting paid by at least two of these categories, and usually by all of them.

How could such a system be anything but a mess? In the polite language of an official Department of Health report, 'there is no framework which allows decisions to be taken in an integrated way that links systematically with the overarching principles of the Irish health care system and aligns resources with goals'.[8] In less polite terms, there are 111,000 people working in a system in which nobody knows what exactly they're trying to achieve. Nobody can set a goal and make sure that resources are allocated in order to reach it.

In fact, the opposite tends to happen. Within this impenetrable system there are what are known in the trade as 'perverse incentives' – rewards for doing the wrong thing. Hospitals are given annual budgets; if they treat more patients than had been envisaged, they exceed those budgets and are penalised. On the other hand, if they stay within budgets by delaying operations, they are rewarded. At the same time, public hospitals have another incentive *not* to treat too many public patients. If they treat a public patient, the money comes out of their budget. If they treat a private patient, they get paid by the health insurance company and it adds to their income.

GPs, meanwhile, are incentivised to set up in wealthier

areas, where they will have fewer medical card patients and can charge higher fees, even though the need for GPs is higher in poorer areas, which have more health problems. In one study, 38 per cent of GPs reported that they needed to work harder in deprived areas to earn the same income.[9]

The supposed aim of health policy is to have more people treated in the community by GPs or primary care teams. But it's often cheaper for a patient to go to hospital than to visit the GP. And while the theoretical attraction of community health services is that they are simple and direct, 'the whole pattern of entitlement to community services', according to the Department of Health's expert group on funding, 'is complex and confusing'.

For private patients, it is often cheaper to try to stay in hospital (where their – very expensive – care is covered by their insurance) than to be discharged back into the care of a GP (whose relatively cheap fees are not covered). As the expert group puts it, 'Once a private patient has been referred to a hospital service, it is in his or her financial interest to avoid being discharged back to primary care.' Equally, private health insurers in many cases fund long hospital stays but do not fund simple mechanisms (like portable machines for applying VAC dressings) that would allow patients to go home earlier.

For hospital consultants, the perversity of the incentives is yet more twisted. A consultant who fails to treat a public patient on his or her waiting list may end up being paid by the National Treatment Purchase Fund for treating that patient in his or her own private practice. It would be wrong to suggest that many consultants deliberately keep public patients waiting so that they can collect private fees for treating them. But that's what the system encourages them to do.

The government's big idea for tackling all of this is to make the Irish system more like the American one, with a push towards the privatisation of services. The problem with this is that the largely private system in the United States is easily the most costly and inefficient in the world. Americans spend almost twice as much per head on health as the Irish do ($7,538 compared to $3,800). In return, the US has fewer physicians per capita than most OECD countries, a smaller number of hospital beds, and life expectancy that is declining relative to the OECD average. It also left 50 million people without health insurance in 2010. One of the reasons for this failure is that for-profit medicine is considerably more expensive than the care that is delivered by public systems.

Yet the Irish government has been doing all in its power to move Ireland in this direction. Apart from copperfastening health apartheid, the drive towards privatisation has been hugely wasteful. The state puts money into private hospitals through tax incentives, but has no idea whether these hospitals make any sense within the overall system. As the Department of Health's own expert group report points out, 'there is a surplus of some types of private hospital space that has developed on foot of subsidies for these investments via the tax system. Unfortunately, despite the tax incentives given, these developments took place in the absence of any integrated health planning structure. Consequently, there is a major challenge ahead to explore how these facilities can be used optimally in the future in light of the very significant state investment in them via tax reliefs.'

Equally, a policy of pushing hospitals to outsource tests to private companies added substantially to costs. Cork University Hospital, for example, discovered in January 2010 that it could save over €200,000 a year on just one test (genetic tests for haemochromatosis) by doing it within the hospital. A private lab in the UK was charging €125 per test. The hospital discovered it could do the test itself for €50. On this one test, the overall annual cost dropped from €265,000 to €35,000.[10]

Ineffective:

The inequities and inefficiencies might be forgiven if the health system was somehow getting the job done. In fact, while it has undoubtedly got better as a result of the huge increases in spending, it has never reached Western European standards. For example, access to medical or surgical specialists is well below the EU27 average, with 49 per cent of Irish respondents reporting easy access, compared to 62 per cent of respondents across the EU. Ireland has nine MRI (magnetic resonance imaging) machines per million of population; the OECD average is thirteen. Ireland has fifteen CT (computed tomography) scanners per million; the OECD average is twenty-four.

From the chaos and squalor of hospital A&E departments to the fact that Ireland has one of the lowest ratios of neurologists per head of population in Europe, the deficits are obvious. But the best way to get a grasp of the ineffectiveness of the system is to consider two of the three main killer diseases: cancer and strokes.

Ireland is second in Europe for the number of cancer cases and deaths from the disease. While death rates for breast cancer have fallen significantly, they are still the second highest in Europe. In 2006 – the most recent figures available – 30.5 women per 100,000 in Ireland died from breast cancer, compared to just 18.9 per 100,000 in Spain.[11] Free vaccination for cervical cancer, a commonplace in most of Europe, is being rolled out in 2010 – but only after the minister for health was forced into a climbdown on the issue. There is still no national risk assessment or genetic screening programme for ovarian cancer in Ireland even though the incidence rate is 22 per cent above the Western European average and the death rate is 37 per cent higher.

And it will take Ireland twenty years on the current strategy to reach European standards of cancer treatment. This is the view, not of an alarmist critic, but of the government's own 'cancer czar'. Professor Tom Keane stated in February 2009 that Ireland ranked close to the bottom in a league table of European countries in terms of five-year cancer survival rates. 'Ireland ranked 18th out of 23 European countries, which was not something to be proud of, he said . . . Professor Keane's goal in reorganising cancer services in the Republic into eight specialist centres was to have Ireland in the top quarter of the EU league table, but he said that could take up to twenty years.'[12]

About 10,000 people have strokes in Ireland every year and over 30,000 people are living with the after-effects of a stroke. In 2008 the Irish Heart Foundation's National Stroke Care Audit concluded that there are up to 500 avoidable deaths in Ireland each year, and thousands of people left unnecessarily with severe disabilities because of the lack of an adequate network of stroke units. It found that 'stroke services in Ireland are so poorly organised that they are largely ineffective'.[1] Specialist stroke units, which are known to be highly effective at saving lives and avoiding severe long-term disabilities, are virtually non-existent – only one Irish hospital has such a unit.

The audit's litany of failures reads like a report on an impoverished developing country:

A tiny fraction of patients who might benefit from acute
interventions such as thrombolysis are assessed for this
therapy. 30 per cent of hospitals did not have routine
access to CT scanning within 48 hours of the stroke
and only 41 per cent had access to emergency MR scanning. Acute rehabilitation is only available to one in four
patients or is delayed beyond the point at which it is
most effective. Continuing care and long-term recovery
programmes are haphazardly organised or do not exist.
The patient journey is not a steady progression through
a seamless and properly organised unitary service. The
quality of care is determined by chance, location and a
haphazard combination of circumstances. The results are
predictable. Too many people die from stroke because
they cannot access optimal treatment sufficiently rapidly.
Too many survivors are left with avoidable and unduly
prolonged disability.

To put 500 unnecessary deaths in context, it is more in one
year than the entire number of deaths in the Northern Ireland conflict between 1989 and 1995.

Yet as well as these dramatic failures, the system is also
ineffective in another sense. It is unable to direct resources to
the places where they will have most effect on well-being –
into preventing illness and keeping people well.

The overall health of Irish people is not as good as it
should be. So called 'healthy life years' are an indicator of the
number of years a person is expected to live in a healthy condition, which is to say, without limitations to their normal
functioning. In 2006 healthy life years stood at 65 for Irish
women and 63.3 for Irish men. The average across the EU15
was estimated at 66 years for women and 64.5 for men.

The Department of Health has estimated that if major risk factors were eliminated and effective interventions applied, 80 per cent of cardiovascular disease and type 2 diabetes, and 40 per cent of cancer, could be avoided. Yet there is no serious effort to deal with these risk factors. Smoking is still relatively heavy, with 29 per cent of the population smoking, compared to the OECD average of 23 per cent. Alcohol consumption in Ireland is among the highest in OECD countries, a full one-third greater than the OECD average. (According to the *Second Report of the Strategic Task Force on Alcohol*, alcohol-related problems cost Irish society in excess of €2.65 billion in 2003 prices.) The percentage of Irish males reporting themselves to be of a healthy weight declined from 48 per cent to 40 per cent between 1998 and 2007. The figures for females declined from 60 per cent to 56 per cent. Yet, apart from the innovative ban on smoking in pubs, nothing is done to tackle these problems, especially if powerful lobby groups are threatened. The government's guidelines of alcohol advertising, for example, were literally written by the drinks industry – the Department of Health cut and pasted the industry's submission and presented the results as public policy.

More broadly, the basic level of healthcare that people can have access to in their own communities is the poor relation of the health service. All the international evidence suggests that countries with comprehensive primary care systems have lower costs and longer life expectancy. But primary care and community health makes up just 10 per cent of the health budget, with a further 5 per cent spent on GP services for medical card holders.

In 2001 the government came up with a primary care strategy based on the idea that 90 to 95 per cent of health and related needs could be met in local centres. When fully developed, the centres would bring together GPs, public health nurses, social workers, practice nurses, midwives, community mental health nurses, dieticians, dentists, community welfare officers, physiotherapists, occupational therapists, home helps, health care assistants, speech and language therapists, chiropodists, community pharmacists and psychologists. A core local team would be supported by a network of more specialised professionals. The plan was to have between 600 and a thousand of these teams. By the beginning of 2010, nine years after the strategy was unfurled, there were just 112 fully functioning teams and 222 in all with some kind of existence, however skeletal.[14] Yet, without these primary care teams in place, nothing else in the Irish health system makes much sense. (The entire hospitals strategy, for example, is predicated on the existence of primary-care teams in the community.) There could be no stronger evidence on which to conclude that the current system is simply incapable of getting to a point where it spends limited resources in the best way. The primary care strategy enjoys wide support, has the potential to be extremely cost-effective in the medium and long term, and combines efficiency and fairness. Perhaps that's why the current system can't cope with it.

The unfairness, inefficiency and ineffectiveness of the health system is the greatest single source of despair about public provision in Ireland. Its bitter divisiveness is the antithesis of republican values. Conversely, a fair, effective and efficient health system would do more than anything else, not just to improve people's lives, but to give them a sense of collective pride and unity of purpose. If this mess can be sorted out, a new health system can be a rallying point for citizens in the way that the creation of the National Health Service was for people in Britain after the Second World War. A decent health service would make the idea of a republic real.

It can be done – and done in the lifetime of one government. We know this because other European countries have done it before – often in circumstances far more miserable than those of post-boom Ireland. The precondition is an agreement that there is no point in tinkering with the current system, and that change has to be radical. But no radical change is likely to work unless it is reasonably simple to understand and delivers tangible benefits quickly.

The only model that can do this is one that achieves two things. One is to ensure that the money follows the patient, rather than, as in the current public system, the other way around. The other is to ensure that people get access to treatment based on the urgency of their need rather than on their ability to pay. Both of these gains can be delivered by what is generally called social health insurance.

There's no great mystery about social health insurance systems. Most countries in Western Europe have one. After the collapse of Communism, the Slovak Republic, the Czech Republic, Poland and Slovenia were able to create social health insurance systems within a few years. There are various models, and it is possible to argue over which one suits Ireland best. But a lot of work has already been done and there are detailed and authoritative proposals on the table from the Adelaide Hospital Society. What follows is essentially a summary of those proposals; those wanting more of the technical detail should read the reports.[15]

The underlying principle of social health insurance is 'access on the basis of clinical need, payment on the basis of income or wealth'. All citizens have insurance cover which entitles them equally to a common 'basket' of services. In relation to what Ireland can afford, this would be free access to primary care, free prescriptions and free access to both in-patient and out-patient hospital services.

Essentially, everyone with an income above a basic threshold would pay into a fund, which would be entirely separate from general exchequer revenues and from taxation. (This is important because it means that the fund is not subject to the cycles of splurging and cutting. Health services can be planned and developed over time.) For those below the income threshold, the state pays the insurance premium.

The beauty of this system is that it abolishes the distinction between private and public patients – and also between private and public hospitals. The fund can contract for services from anyone who meets the necessary standards of care. Crucially, healthcare providers have to compete for the patient's money – instead of the current situation in which patients effectively have to compete with each other to get into the system. Instead of the current incentive *not* to treat patients, hospitals would get paid only when they actually treated someone.

This system gets rid of all the 'perverse incentives' that bedevil Irish healthcare at the moment. There is no playing around with public patients on long waiting lists whose consultants are then paid by the state to treat them as private patients. There is no bonus for GPs to work in better-off areas – everyone has the same entitlement to GP services. There are no deterrents to people using the simplest and most cost-effective services (primary care) first.

The system is transparent: people can see exactly what they're getting for what they're paying. It is far simpler than the current plethora of different models – and simplicity makes accountability possible. It is much less bureaucratic: a great deal of what the HSE does would be made redundant, as would the National Treatment Purchase Fund, which cost €90 million in 2009. The governance of the health system can be greatly simplified, with responsibility for the primary care strategy going to the new local authorities and a slimmed-down HSE concentrating on strategic and infrastructural issues. The immensely complicated question of 'risk equalisation' between private health insurance companies becomes redundant. (People may still wish to take out private insurance to cover things which are not in the common 'basket' of services, but the basic questions of fairness between generations no longer arise.)

Is this system affordable in straitened times? Yes – the overall cost would be similar to the current system. The cost of 'levelling up' everyone to the kind of services that those with private insurance currently enjoy would be about 3 per cent extra deduction from incomes. A single person on €25,000 would pay an additional amount of €20 per month for a single-tier system with good access to comprehensive primary and acute care and would no longer pay fees for GPs, hospital services or drugs.

In fact, if the system is run efficiently and manages to make a saving of 20 per cent on current costs, it may not have any extra cost at all. The potential for such savings is real. Contracting for services rather than doling out annual budgets would give providers incentives to deliver services more effectively. The large bureaucracy currently in place would be slimmed down. People would use their community health services more often, resulting in earlier diagnosis and less expensive treatments (as well as, of course, in better chances of recovery.)

There is plenty of scope for making health services cheaper and better at the same time. Proper stroke units would save lives, but also result in fewer people requiring long-term care for debilitating conditions. Better facilities in the community and better support for home carers can keep people in their own homes at a fraction of the cost of putting them into hospitals and institutions. (The TCD report entitled *There is No Place like Home* found that it is nine times more expensive to provide acute hospital care for children with severe intellectual and physical disabilities than to have them cared for at home.)[16]

One way to bring down the costs of GP services is, paradoxically, to increase the number of GPs. Ireland severely restricts the number of Irish graduates from medical schools to 121 a year, which ensures that the demand for GP services outstrips the supply. The number of GPs per head of population is only about 60 per cent of what it is in many European countries.

Perhaps most importantly, investment in preventive medicine and in tackling Ireland's deep problems with alcohol, tobacco and obesity would pay enormous personal, social and financial dividends. So, too, would a recognition of that €6 billion a year that the health effects of inequality costs us. Turning the sickness system into a genuine health system would improve the level of well-being in Ireland far more than an abstract rise in GDP. It would also create one of the basic conditions of a republic – the belief that the lives of all of its citizens are of equal value.

3
A Smart Society:
The Decency of Education

The *Growing Up in Ireland* study is a large-scale national project tracking the progress of 18,500 children over seven years. In its first snapshot of nine-year-old kids, it found that most of them were broadly happy at school. But it also found something rather striking. Even at this tender age, the scores that these kids were getting for reading and maths were very heavily influenced by their mother's level of education. The kids' scores went down just as their mothers' level of education declined. Kids whose mothers were graduates scored 63 and 78 in maths and vocabulary respectively. Kids whose mothers had only lower secondary education scored 45 and 59. In a real sense these children are being taught, not just by their present teachers, but by those who taught – or failed to teach – their mothers.[1]

As James Williams and Sheila Greene, who analysed the study, concluded:

Academic success, even at nine years of age, was strongly related to the child's socio-economic circumstances . . . children whose mother was herself less well educated were much more likely to be in the lowest reading quintile than were the children of graduate mothers (30 per cent compared with 8 per cent). The corollary, of course

. . . shows that 36 per cent of children whose mother is a graduate were in the highest reading quintile, compared with 11 per cent of those whose mother left school at lower secondary level or less. The pattern for other aspects of social background (income, social class, etc.) was consistent with that for maternal education. The pattern of children's performance in Maths was very similar to that in reading. In general, children from higher social class backgrounds, income categories and maternal education groups had a much higher chance of being in the highest quintile of scores on the Maths test.[2]

In other words, even at the age of nine there are clear winners and losers in the Irish educational system. And the reasons why some children are disadvantaged are clear enough. There is no mystery about the fact that better-educated parents are more likely to be able to give their children an environment rich in intellectual stimulation and to help them with problems at school. But the children of more poorly educated mothers were also found to have been absent from school more often (7.6 days in the previous year, compared to 5.4 days for those from well-educated households). They are also more likely to be sick: 76 per cent of nine-year-olds from professional/managerial groups were reported to be 'very healthy', compared with 69 per cent of those from semi-skilled/unskilled manual backgrounds. And they are almost three times more likely to be obese: 11 per cent compared to 4 per cent. This suggests that the kids from better-educated backgrounds are better fed and have more access to sport and play.

If you read current official strategy documents, you will discover that the plan is to get more than half of these struggling nine-year-olds into third-level education in a decade's time. This intention is not driven purely by an altruistic belief in equality, or by the notion that a republic ought not to be able to stomach the idea that the winners and losers in its education system have already been pretty much chosen at the age of nine. It is driven, above all, by collective self-interest. If Ireland is to have a successful economy in 2020, it will be one in which levels of education are outstandingly high. That means, according to the National Skills Strategy, having around three-quarters of young people participating in higher education. And that, in turn means getting over half of the poorer socio-economic groups into third-level colleges.

Which raises the obvious question: how likely is this to happen to the nine-year-olds who are already so far behind their peers?

There is pretty much universal agreement that the single most important factor in making Ireland prosperous in the 1990s was not low corporate taxation or EU money or social partnership, but education. To a large extent the boom was shaped by a radical shift in education policy – the belated introduction of free secondary education in 1967. By greatly widening the pool of people with sufficient education to develop high-level skills, Ireland became highly attractive to companies looking for skilled labour. In 2008 34 per cent of the Irish labour force had completed some form of higher education, compared to just 4 per cent in the early 1970s.

The problem with this achievement is that it can't be a once-off shift. A quantum leap of a similar scale will be needed if Ireland's ambitions of being a 'smart economy' are to be fulfilled. Everybody else wants to have a smart economy too – the standards are being raised all the time.

Looked at in the most brutally mechanistic way, it is probably true to say that the Ireland of the last twenty years could just about afford to leave behind the equivalent of our nine-year-olds. Doing so may have been deeply unjust and shameful, but Ireland could get away with it because the middle and upper classes were extremely good at taking advantage of the new educational opportunities. Social injustice has not prevented Ireland from improving the overall levels of education.

First, second-level education expanded rapidly: full-time enrolments have grown from under 41,000 in 1980 to almost 140,000 today. Then the same thing happened at third level: the entry rate to higher education has grown from 20 per cent of school leavers in 1980 to a current rate of approximately 55 per cent. These are genuine achievements and the institutions deserve great credit for managing this quick expansion without seriously compromising standards.

However hard this transformation was, though, it was the easy part. Rates of participation among the middle and upper classes are now pretty much at saturation point. Children of higher professionals reached what is effectively full participation in 1998 and have maintained that situation ever since. Farming households have participation approaching 90 per cent. About two-thirds of 17–18 year olds from households headed by lower professionals, employers, managers and the self-employed now enter higher education. There are certainly gains to be made in these latter groups, but they will have a limited impact on the overall goals.

A large-scale further expansion of educational attainment, of the kind that Ireland will need in the next decade if it is to be a world-class knowledge economy, cannot come from the social groups who are already fully plugged into the system. It has to come from those who have been left behind. In essence, the big challenge in upskilling the Irish population lies with two groups – those who are not currently getting to third level and those older workers who have relatively low skills and levels of education. In other words, Ireland can't close its skills gap unless it closes its social justice gap. A system of education that's fit for a smart economy would also be one that's fit for a republic.

With those currently in the workforce, Ireland has a particular problem. Because free secondary education was introduced so late relative to other European countries, there is still a large proportion of the workforce that has only primary or lower secondary schooling. In the 55–64 age group, 42 per cent of people have only primary education. In the 45–54 age group, 44 per cent of people have only a lower secondary education or worse. And even in the 25–34 age group, 18 per cent have been educated only as far as the Junior Certificate or worse.

This education gap makes it all the more important for Ireland to be at the forefront of adult education and lifelong learning. Instead, it is near the back of the class. Eurostat data indicates that in 2007, 7.6 per cent of the Irish population aged between twenty-five and sixty-four were in receipt of education in the previous four weeks, compared to an EU15 average of 12 per cent. In 2004 the participation rate for Irish adults of the same age group in education and training was estimated at 7 per cent. This compared with an EU25 average of 10 per cent and participation rates of between 25 per cent and 36 per cent among the Scandinavians.

The situation is actually worse than these figures suggest. Most of those taking part in adult education and training are not those who lost out on education in the first place. Irish adults with third-level qualifications are almost four times more likely to participate in continuing education and training than their peers with less than upper-second-level education. In this sense, adult education mirrors the rest of the system – those who need it most are least likely to get it.

One radical way of thinking about this problem, and indeed about educational equality in general, is to adopt a system of individual educational funds. The current funding of education means that those who get most education – who tend to be better off already – get most money spent on them by the state, and those who are poorest get least. A way to rethink this would be to assign everyone at birth an educational fund equivalent to, say, the cost of their education up to primary degree level. This fund could be drawn down at any time in the life cycle. Thus those who miss out on education in youth would have the incentive of knowing that there is a large part of their fund still waiting for them to spend on appropriate improvements to their skills. Detailed costings would need to be drawn up, but ideas of this kind have to be explored seriously if the goals of upskilling the population as a whole are to be achieved.

In relation to the other key group – today's disadvantaged nine-year-olds – it is worth noting that even the relatively ambitious official strategy is a plan for a continuation of large-scale inequality. The National Plan for Equity of Access to Higher Education sets the overall target of getting the percentage of school leavers who go on to higher education up from the present 55 per cent to 72 per cent in 2020. But its target for the lower socio-economic groups is not 72 per cent. It is 'at least 54 per cent'. In other words, even if the plan works, kids from poorer backgrounds will be in 2020 where their peers from better-off backgrounds are now. As revolutions go, this is not the storming of the Bastille but a polite knock on the door.

But even this very timid goal is wildly unrealistic if things stay broadly as they are. Consider how far there is to go in order to get every social class in Ireland with a participation rate for higher education of at least 54 per cent. At the moment, three classes are below this figure: the 'skilled manual' at 50 per cent; the 'semi- and unskilled manual' at 33 per cent and the so-called 'non-manual' at 27 per cent. It is reasonable to assume that the children of skilled manual workers will reach the target. But for the other two groups to make it there will have to be a radical change, not just in education policy, but in the nature of Irish society.

Let's look at the current situation. In the academic year 2008–9 (the latest for which figures are available), the largest socio-economic group for new entrants to both universities and institutes of technology was 'employer and manager'. In the universities, 21 per cent of all new undergraduates came from this small section of society. And this proportion was actually an increase on the previous year. Far from becoming less dominant, the upper class is becoming more so. If even the modest goals that have been set for increasing the overall levels of education in Irish society are to be attained, this trend has to be reversed.

It is, of course, not at all surprising that the better-off would tighten their grip on higher education in the midst of an economic crisis. They know very well that there is a very strong relationship between education and income. Income levels increase in line with the educational level of the head of household. Households headed by a person with a third-level degree or above had a net disposable household income of €75,686 in 2008. This compares with households headed by a person with a lower secondary or below education who had a net disposable household income of €31,595.[3] Almost

69 per cent of those with a third-level degree or higher were in the top 30 per cent of income earners, compared with just under 10 per cent of those with a lower secondary education or below. The image of the self-made man (it is almost always a man) who left school at fourteen and became a billionaire is much loved, but it bears little relation to the big picture.

Even to get to the modest level of 54 per cent participation by 2020, the leap that has to be made by those groups who currently fare worst in the system is huge. To get the semi- and unskilled group up to that level by then, it will have to reach an interim target of 45 per cent by 2013 – up 12 percentage points in the next two years. This would be a stunning achievement, considering that in the best of times, when opportunities abounded, the rate of participation by this group rose by 10 per cent between 1998 and 2004. The improvement will have to be significantly larger in two lean years than it was in six good ones. Given what is actually planned to happen in the next two years, with further cutbacks in education and social spending that are certain to have the biggest effect on the worst off, who's kidding who?

If we're serious about either social justice or the smart economy, we have to start by considering two obvious things. The first is money. It matters. One of the interesting things about the inequalities in entry to higher education is that the worst-affected group is not the traditional working class in the semi- and unskilled manual category. It is the strange ragbag that is the 'non-manual class'. While the children of manual workers have a participation rate of 33 per cent, the non-manual are at just 27 per cent.

Who are these people? For a start they're about a fifth of the population. Some of them are the children of reasonably high-status parents, such as Garda sergeants, and they actually get to third level in decent numbers. But the bulk of the group is made up of what might be called the lower middle class – clerical and office workers, minor central and local government officials, sales people and retail workers, child-care workers. How come they're at the bottom of the heap? Because they're caught in the middle – too well-off to qualify for grants and too poor to be able to afford to send their kids to college without grants. As the Higher Education Authority puts it, 'many families within the non-manual sector have an income level that disqualifies them from accessing grants currently even though such income levels are clearly inadequate to allow participation in higher education'.[4]

For all the talk of 'culture' as a barrier to higher education, the barrier these kids have to climb is made of euro notes. They need more financial help than the current grant system provides. The average cost for a young person going to college is €7,000 a year. Even for those lucky enough to qualify for a grant, it will cover at best half this cost. As the HEA acknowledges, 'In the design of the maintenance grants system, there is a presumption of parental support for higher-education students and the grant is intended to supplement this support where the reckonable household income falls below certain levels . . . the standard rate of the . . . grant covers roughly half of the average (median) costs of participation.'

Where is the money to raise the grants to a decent level (effectively to double them) to come from? There are two stark options – either raise taxes specifically for this purpose or shift the money that is currently spent on free college fees. (This question is separate from the broader crisis in the funding of higher education.) The case for the state continuing to pay the college fees for students from the highest income brackets while those from poorer families are denied access to higher education is extremely weak.

The link between universities and fee-paying schools, on the other hand, is very strong. In 2008 a fifth of all university students had paid fees at second level.[5] At the country's largest university, UCD, the link was even stronger – 43 per cent of students came from either fee-paying or grind schools, offering private tuition to supplement the ordinary preparation for state exams. There is surely an irony in the state paying third-level fees for those whose parents could, and did, pay fees for them at second level, when free options were available. This anomaly reflects a phenomenon that raises fundamental questions about the wisdom of free university fees for the well-off. When university fees were abolished, many upper middle-class parents simply used the money they would have spent on them to send their children to private secondary schools. Enrolment in many good free schools, including long-established institutions such as Synge Street and St Joseph's CBS in Dublin, dried up. Some schools, such as Presentation in Glasthule, Dublin, and Greendale Community School in north Dublin, were even forced to close because of falling numbers. By contrast, fee-paying schools in the same areas could not cope with demand and had long waiting lists for entry.

Essentially, what the state ended up doing was the opposite of its intention. The purpose of a blanket abolition of third-level fees was to make the education system fairer – but the effect was that the state ended up indirectly subsidising the fees of pupils attending fee-paying secondary schools so that they could consolidate their already formidable advantages.

It has often been pointed out that these private schools are subsidised to the tune of €100 million a year by the state, which pays their teachers. In reality the subsidy is much greater. Many of the 26,000 pupils enrolled in the State's fifty-one fee-paying schools and paying €6,000 a year as day pupils are having a large slice of that fee paid out of money that would otherwise have been spent on their university education. The Department of Finance backed a 50 per cent cut in state support for fee-paying schools in 2008, pointing out that savings of €47 million could be achieved by cutting the number of teachers paid for by the state. The proposals were dismissed by the government. But if there is any seriousness about increasing the number of students from less privileged social groups, these subsidies (both direct and indirect) should be ended and the money channelled towards increases in the maintenance grant.

Money, however, is not the only issue. While there are students who would go to third-level colleges if they could afford it, there are many others who don't ever get to a point where such a choice really exists. Long-term educational disadvantage is structural. It is shaped by poverty, both financial and cultural; by housing and healthcare; by long-term unemployment and by the educational levels of parents. No education system on its own can transform all of these conditions. But it can have a damn good try.

The problem of getting more working-class students into higher education is a Babushka doll. Inside it there is the problem of secondary-school dropouts, inside that there is the problem of primary school failure and inside that there is the problem of early childhood care and education.

The level of dropout from secondary school has remained virtually unchanged since the late 1980s. Between 1992 and 2004 second-level completion rates stuck at 82 per cent. The most recent data estimate that there has been a slight improvement, with approximately 84 per cent of pupils now completing second-level education. A 2 per cent rise in eighteen years is not a rate of progress that is going to see any of the smart economy targets being met. The National Skills Strategy envisages a retention rate of at least 90 per cent by 2020 – a much faster rate of progress than the system has actually managed. There needs to be a radical reappraisal of the secondary education system, in which everything, including the domination of the entire curriculum by preparation for the Leaving Certificate, is on the table. It is clear that the system is failing in some areas of knowledge – why, for example, do over 40 per cent of students taking higher mathematics take extra tuition outside of school? – but it seems also to fail some kinds of students.

This in turn brings us back to our nine-year-olds. If they are already at a serious disadvantage, what is the primary school system doing about it? Many teachers make heroic efforts, but by any standards primary education is woefully under-resourced. For every €6 spent at primary, €9 is spent at second level and €12 is spent at third level. In 2003 OECD countries spent an average of €88,000 on children up to the age of eighteen; the Irish spend was €81,000, and the difference was most pronounced for the youngest children. Irish primary schools have 24.5 pupils per class – the second largest of the EU countries surveyed. On average, there are four more pupils in Irish classes than in other EU countries. There are over 100,000 primary school children in class sizes of thirty or more.

In relation to the nine-year-olds in the *Growing Up in Ireland* survey, nearly a quarter (23 per cent) of them were attending schools in which the principal felt there was an inadequate number of classrooms. A substantial proportion of nine-year-olds were in schools in which the principal felt that facilities for children with disabilities (24 per cent), library facilities (37 per cent) and after-school facilities (41 per cent) were poor. The poverty of all of these facilities is likely to have a disproportionate effect on the weaker students, who depend more on school for their development.

The reality is that current levels of commitment to primary education are failing to bridge the gap between the advantaged and the disadvantaged. The National Competiveness Council notes that 'the relative performance of pupils in designated disadvantaged schools has shown no improvement' between 1999 and 2004.[6]

And behind primary education, there is early childhood education, a field in which Ireland has an atrocious record. The National Competiveness Council, looking at the issue from a purely economic point of view, nevertheless notes that pre-primary education is 'considered the most important level of education in an individual's cognitive development'. It said that 'Investing in pre-primary or early childhood education and care is a unique opportunity for public policy to promote social justice and productivity in the economy at the same time.'

In 2008 Unicef published a report card on early childhood education in twenty-five OECD countries. It ranked Ireland twenty-fifth. Of ten benchmarks for quality, Ireland met one.[7] Since then there has been a significant and welcome development in the establishment of a free pre-school year for all children. The key questions are whether high standards can be established, maintained and made universal, and whether commitment to pre-primary education will survive a government strategy of slashing public spending.

The unavoidable conclusion is that Ireland has to spend a

lot more money on education and target it a lot more ruth-
lessly at those who need help most. And unlike other areas,
this is not one in which better outcomes can be achieved by
spending about the same as we currently do. The Irish education system is already efficient in terms of processing very
large numbers of young people at relatively low cost. In this
case, less is not more. More is.

On the other hand, though, the potential economic benefits are higher than in any other area. Money well spent
on education, especially for the disadvantaged, saves much
more money later on.

A National Economic and Social Forum (NESF) cost-
benefit analysis in 2005 showed that for every euro invested in early childhood education in Ireland, a return of up
to €7.10 could be expected. A report by the KPMG foundation in the UK found that the cost to the exchequer of
pupils leaving school with low literacy is between £44,797
and £53,098 per pupil over half a lifetime: an annual cost of
£1.7–2.5 billion. The return on investment in early interventions in reading skills would be between £14.81 and £17.56
on every pound.

An ESRI report in 2009 assessed the costs associated with
early school leaving in the Irish context. They estimate that
the cost to the state in jobseeker's allowance over a lifetime
for an average male early school leaver is €12,300. Lost
tax amounts to €17,000, making a loss of €29,300, before
health or crime costs are considered.

More positively, though, the long-term economic benefits
of raising educational standards are staggering. The OECD
has calculated that an increase of 25 points on PISA educational testing scores would increase GDP in Ireland by $514
billion between now and 2090. If Ireland were brought to the

same educational level as Finland, the value would be $870 billion – 453 per cent of current GDP.[8]

The truth that has to be grasped is that there is no smart economy without a smart society. And smart societies don't waste their human wealth by putting up with systems in which nine-year-olds can be labelled as failures because of the dumb luck of the social class into which they happened to be born.

4

Beyond the Ultimatum Game:
The Decency of Equality

Suppose I were to give you €1,000 on certain simple conditions. You have to share it with a stranger. You can offer them as much, or as little, of the money as you like. If the stranger, who knows the rules and how much I've given you, accepts your offer, both of you can keep the agreed sums. But if the stranger rejects the offer, I get the money back and you both walk away with nothing. There is no haggling and no second chance – you make the offer and the stranger decides whether to accept it or walk away empty-handed.

This is actually a standard behavioural experiment called the Ultimatum Game, invented in the early 1980s by the German sociologist Werner Guth.[1] It has been played thousands of times in many different cultures – in Asia, Europe and America, in isolated tribal societies and in cyberspace, in rich and poor countries – and the results are always broadly the same. And they are not what they teach on almost any economics course.

Standard economic models would suggest that the stranger simply has to take whatever you offer since, say, €200 of the €1,000 is much better than the sweet FA that results from saying 'no'. They would also suggest that it makes sense for you to make a low offer, since you know that the stranger has a choice between something and nothing.

In fact, this is not what happens. Most of those given the money don't make low offers – the most common is 50 per cent, or €500 in this case. Anything below €300 is highly unusual. Even more interestingly, most of the strangers will not accept anything less than €300, very few will accept less than €200 and many will walk away from anything less than €500. They will flatly turn down, say, a free €250 because they don't like being exploited or treated unfairly. 'The response to a miserly take-it-or-leave it ultimatum is "you can keep it".'

People will actually sacrifice their narrowly defined economic self-interest if they feel they're being cheated or taken for a ride. Even when the sums of money are very large (one test in Indonesia involved an offer of three months' income but the average offer was still 42 per cent of the total sum), justice matters at least as much as the money does. Even when the experiment is done online, and the participants interact anonymously, people will not trade for money the dignity they get from being treated with fairness and respect. Or to put it more negatively, we're damned if we're going to let some brass-necked chancer walk away with the bulk of the cash, even if we have to take an economic hit ourselves to make sure they don't.

Ireland at the moment is one giant Ultimatum Game, with the unfortunate twist that what is being shared out is not free money but what are euphemistically known as 'sacrifices'. The society as a whole has to understand that there is a lot less money around than there used to be. It has to do that in the context of entirely justified rage at the breathtaking unfairness of a banking bailout in which the working and middle classes will be paying, year after year, for the gambling debts of their betters. If it is to emerge from this gruelling process with any sense of shared interests left intact, it is crucial that the offer that is being made is a fair one. Otherwise, more and more people will – in one form or another – walk away from the table.

Right-wing economics of the kind that has been dominant in Ireland makes much of 'human nature', which is always assumed to be essentially selfish and driven by a relentless desire to accumulate riches and power. But human nature also includes a dread of inferiority. As social animals, we are conditioned to feel a deep fear at the prospect of being left outside the group. This dread has economic effects. Arguably, much of the manic spending of the boom years in Ireland was driven by a desperate need not to be seen to fall behind, to be missing out, to be inferior. Equality made itself felt – through its absence. And the economic effects were disastrous. A society which is able to behave more rationally in economic terms will be one in which there is no great dread of inferiority because there is no flaunting of superiority. It will, in other words, be one that makes its theoretical commitment to equality real.

There is, therefore, a more positive way to look at the challenge of sharing out the sacrifices. The innate sense of fairness that people have in all cultures translates, in political terms, into the idea of equality. That idea is at the core of any meaningful notion of what a republic is. It is also crucial to the general level of well-being in society. Equality is the glue that binds together politics and economics. And in the way it adapts to the crisis, Ireland can emerge as a much more equal society.

One of the things that has happened as a result of the collapse of the boomtime economy is that Irish people have become much more conscious of inequality. Most already had few illusions about the reality of their society, but awareness of the disparities in the distribution of wealth has increased sharply in the aftermath of the crash. In a Tasc/Behaviour and Attitudes survey in 2008, 70 per cent of people said that wealth is distributed not very or not at all fairly in Ireland, while 29 per cent thought it was distributed quite or very fairly. In the same survey in 2010, the 'not very/not at all' group had risen to 87 per cent and the 'quite/ very' group had fallen to just 12 per cent.[2]

This finding is not surprising. Irish people have had a crash course in the nature of self-serving elites. They have learned – too late, alas – that the justifications for lavish salaries and expenses for the 'best people' in politics, banking, regulatory agencies and the professions were hollow. If there was any relationship between what people were paid and the good they did for society as a whole, it was generally an inverse one – the more extravagant the salary, the greater and more destructive the incompetence. But they have also seen how extraordinarily resilient those elites are, how quickly and shamelessly they reverted to the notion that no self-respecting patriot could be expected to get out of bed for less than €250,000 a year plus a pot of gold at the end of the pension rainbow. Instead of boiling away in simmering rage, though, this awareness needs to be channelled into a constructive determination to emerge from this grim period with the prize of a more equal – and therefore more sustainable – society.

In 2008 the disposable weekly income of the top 10 per cent in Ireland was €2,451, eleven and a half times that of the bottom 10 per cent, which had €215 a week.[3] Ireland had the highest level of earnings inequality of the original fifteen EU countries.[4] The inevitable accompaniment of this gulf in incomes is a high level of relative poverty. At the end of the boom, 14.4 per cent of the population, and 18 per cent of children, were at risk of poverty. These figures are likely to have become significantly worse, given both the cuts in welfare payments and other public spending in the last three budgets and wage cuts for low-paid workers.

In the US in 1980 the average chief executive took home roughly forty times the average industrial wage; by 2001 chief executive pay packages were about 350 times the wage of a typical worker. Ireland followed this trend, albeit somewhat more slowly. By 2007 the average remuneration packages granted to the top twenty chief executives of Irish public companies were thirty-five times higher than the annual income of the average employee.[5]

As in the other Anglo-Saxon economies, the boom years saw those in positions of power in Ireland make a shameless lunge towards the feeding trough. Pay for those at the top has risen far faster than for the average worker. The average pay for CEOs in private companies rose by 46 per cent in the two years between 2005 and 2007; pay for CEOs in state companies rose by 42 per cent in the same period. Yet during those years, average gross incomes rose by just 17.5 per cent. CEOs were paid 110 times the threshold below which people are judged to be 'at risk of poverty' – one in six Irish households was below this threshold in those years.[6]

This process was helped along by a very convenient coincidence: the 'top people' often had the pleasant task of deciding on each other's pay. The Tasc report Mapping the Golden Circle gives an example of the way, in 2007, the remuneration committees of four of the largest Irish companies – Anglo Irish Bank, Smurfit, Greencore and McInerney Holdings – were connected through just four individuals with overlapping board memberships: Seán FitzPatrick, Ann

Heraty, Gary McCann and Ned Sullivan. (Seán FitzPatrick, Ann Heraty and Gary McCann were members of the remuneration committee of Anglo Irish Bank that set the payment for the chairperson, Seán FitzPatrick – who in turn, as chair, was involved in setting the remuneration of non-executive directors, who included Ann Heraty and Gary McCann. As chair of Smurfit and a member of the remuneration committee, FitzPatrick was involved in setting the remuneration of the CEO, Gary McCann. FitzPatrick was also a member of the remuneration committee of Greencore, which set the remuneration of the chair Ned Sullivan. Sullivan was a member of the remuneration committees of both Greencore and McInerney Holdings.)

The culture of massive salaries was imported from the private sector into the public sector, in the process virtually destroying an idea that is essential to a republic – the notion that people in positions of leadership have the privilege of serving the public. In 2007 the Review Body on Higher Remuneration in the Public Sector recommended that the Taoiseach's annual salary be raised from €271,822 to €310,000, while proposing that the pay of ministers be lifted from €214,344 to €240,000. The salaries of heads of universities were increased from €226,895 to €270,000, while the review also recommended increases of more than €45,000, to €247,000, for the chief executives of the State agencies Fás, Enterprise Ireland and Forfás.

Perhaps more damaging even than the growing gap between ordinary workers and executives was the breaking of any link between achievement and remuneration. For all the pieties about 'rewarding success', failure didn't turn out to be too unrewarding either. In 2008 Fyffes's chairman David McCann's total pay package increased by 36 per cent, even though the fruit importer's operations lost €1.4 million that year, partly on the back of a €28.6 million hit from its property investment associate, Blackrock International. McCann earned €1.12 million in salary, bonuses and other payments, up from €821,000 a year earlier. Michael Fingleton of Irish Nationwide Building Society was paid a bonus of €1 million just weeks after the government bailed out his operation at a cost of billions to the taxpayer. Alan Merriman, who resigned as finance director of Educational Building Society in March 2009 after the society made a loss of €38.2 million for 2008, received a total package of €479,700 for that year.

This culture was so deeply ingrained that in late September 2008, after the collapse of the banking system, the Fine Gael spokesman on finance Richard Bruton and government minister Willie O'Dea were completely at one in rejecting the notion of a salary cap on banking executives. Bruton suggested that 'If you end up with executives that you need to operate this, moving out of their position to well-paid positions elsewhere, and we're left without the people that we need to run the system, that wouldn't be good.' Willie O'Dea chimed in with: 'There's a practical difficulty here . . . You need to ensure in the interests of the taxpayer that the best people run these institutions.' It was hard to tell which proposition was more ludicrous – that international firms were queuing up to offer the geniuses who ran the Irish banking system 'well-paid positions elsewhere' or that it was 'in the interests of the taxpayer' that these 'best people' remain in charge.

The instinctive nature of these attitudes among so many members of the political class ensured that the huge increase in executive salaries during the boom has been rolled back only a little since the crisis began. The average pay of chief executives in Irish public companies fell in 2009 from €1.3

million to €936,000; the average total package for a non-executive chairman fell even more gently, from €161,000 to €149,000.

Even in the banks into which the taxes paid by ordinary workers are being shovelled, austerity comes in a golden casket. The aptly named Richie Boucher, chief executive of Bank of Ireland, has a salary of €623,000. Allied Irish Bank paid out almost €3.6 million to directors in 2009, down from €5 million in 2008 but not bad for an institution that lost €2.65 billion in 2009. In Anglo Irish Bank, which recorded the biggest banking loss in the world in 2009 – twice the losses of the giant US lender Citigroup – fees for directors actually went up in that year of glory: the chairman's fee was increased from €218,000 to €250,000, while non-executive directors' fees were increased from €44,000 to €73,000. Nama, meanwhile, has set aside a budget of €2.4 *billion* over ten years for professional fees, making it in effect a luxury public works scheme for lawyers, valuers and accountants.

It is clear that most Irish people no longer find acceptable the notion that the 'best people' should earn thirty-five times more than mere toilers at the coalface. The Tasc/Behaviour and Attitudes survey found very strong support for the idea that government should take active steps to reduce the gap between high and low earners, with 91 per cent agreeing with this proposition. This level of consensus presents a real opportunity for a once-in-a-generation sea change in Irish culture, with a steady and progressive shift away from the glorification of greed and towards economic equality.

The first aspect of this change is an attack on the idea that sustains inequality – the notion that economic inequalities are the outcome of 'natural' differences in human ability. It may seem hard to have to take this idea seriously, since its proponents almost never do so. They never tell us how, for example, Seán FitzPatrick's abilities are a thousand times more valuable than those of a firefighter who saves people's lives or a carer who gives dignity to a fellow human being. Nor do they ever follow through on their own supposed beliefs and argue for the seizure of inherited wealth – a position that ought to appeal to them since they allegedly believe that merit would assert itself without such advantages.

And they inevitably draw their examples, not from the real world that the vast majority of people inhabit, but from the fantasy worlds of entertainment and sport. 'We can't all have Marlene Dietrich's legs,' argues Milton Friedman. 'It's like a football team,' says Mary Harney. 'Some make premier division and others aren't so good, unfortunately' – as if Michael Fingleton got a €23 million pension pot because he looks good in silk stockings or a kid in a Nairobi shanty town lives in a tin hut with a dirt floor merely because he can't play football like Didier Drogba.

The truth is that high levels of income inequality don't encourage people to develop their talents and don't enable economic growth. They have precisely the opposite effect. As OECD Secretary-General Angel Gurría – hardly a communist – put it:

> The OECD looked at links between inequality and growth. We found no evidence that inequality may be conducive to growth in OECD countries, as some had suggested . . . On the contrary, our work shows that greater income inequality stifles upward mobility between generations, making it harder for talented and hardworking people to get the rewards they deserve. And the resulting inequality of opportunities, the lack of 'social

capillarity', inevitably impacts economic performance as a whole.[7]

The flimsy arguments for inequality are based on a crude misunderstanding of genetics and IQ. People, the story goes, are born with innate, genetically determined differences in intelligence. It is these differences that work their way through over a lifetime into disparities of achievement and therefore of wealth. This cod science needs to be challenged. Genes don't 'determine' something as complex as intelligence – in the broad sense, genes don't determine anything much. They create sets of possibilities which may or not develop, depending on a range of environmental factors. We evolved to be extremely flexible creatures – our brains are shaped by our experiences of the world.

'Intelligence' is a subjective idea that changes according to time and situation. A good definition is that of Howard Gardner: 'An intelligence is the ability to solve problems, or to create products, that are valued within one or more cultural settings.'[8] There are numerous kinds of intelligence: Gardner suggested seven; others have suggested nine. The present author, for example, is supposedly smart enough to write books and a newspaper column, but cannot drive a car, change a plug or milk a cow, and once failed an aptitude test to become a guard on the Tube in London. Judgements of intelligence depend entirely on what is valued. And they change radically over time. As Daniel Dorling points out, 'the average child in 1900 measured by today's standards would appear to be an imbecile'.

Nor do IQ tests measure intelligence in any kind of objective way. They are rigged to produce a preconceived distribution of results, with bell curves that determine there will be a very few at the top, a bunching in the middle, and a few at the bottom. These curves produce bizarre results: most children are determined to be quite dull. In the Netherlands, for example, just 39 per cent are supposed to be functioning beyond the level of 'simple' intelligence and 34 per cent are supposed to have no intelligence, limited intelligence or barely adequate intelligence.[9] Why? Because the tests are calibrated to support the assumption that most children are consigned to failure or mediocrity and that only a small elite will ever get to be as smart as the kind of people who devise IQ tests. All such pseudo-scientific justifications for inequality should be dumped. We need to accept that being equal is an entirely different concept to being the same, and to start thinking about a society in which everyone has the opportunity to develop his or her abilities.

Attempts to destroy even the minimal protection that the weaker members of the workforce currently have must be resisted. The employers' group Ibec claims that the minimum wage is 'clearly part of Ireland's overall competitiveness disadvantage' and there has been a deluge of claims that the wages of ordinary workers are uncompetitive in an international context. If this campaign succeeds, income disparities will actually widen. There is clearly no intention to substantially reduce the incomes of very high earners, so cutting those lower down the scale will increase inequality.

How well grounded are these claims? The most recent National Competitiveness Report gives the lie to the notion that wage levels in Ireland are out of line with those in other Western European countries:

Ireland has the tenth highest total labour costs level in the OECD and is in line with a number of Western European

countries . . . wage costs for unskilled and skilled production operatives working in internationally trading
business in Ireland are close to the euro area average
. . . [while] Irish wage levels remain significantly below
those of other high income countries like Germany and
Denmark . . . Growth rates in Irish labour costs slowed
significantly in 2008 and the first half of 2009 and were
lower than the EU-27 and euro area-6 average.

Specific attacks on the minimum wage, meanwhile, cite
claims that Ireland has the highest or second highest minimum wage in Europe. These claims are simply untrue. Eurostat did produce figures in 2009 that seemed to show that
Ireland has the second highest minimum wage after Luxembourg, and these were seized on by right-wing commentators. They ignored Eurostat's adjusted figures that showed
that, in terms of purchasing power, the Irish rate is the sixth
highest in the EU, behind Luxembourg, the Netherlands,
Belgium, France and the UK. Judged as a percentage of the
average industrial wage, Ireland's €8.65 an hour falls to sev-
enth highest in the EU.

But even these figures are somewhat misleading. A number
of countries have lower statutory minimum wage levels but,
as the Competitiveness Report puts it, 'operate non-statutory
minimum wage rates on a sectoral basis and have rates which
are significantly higher than Ireland's'.

The only economic effect of further impoverishing those
who are already struggling would be to give the downward
spiral of deflation another twist. A 39-hour working week
on the minimum wage currently provides an income of €337
euro. According to research undertaken by the Vincentian
Partnership in 2009, a worker with a non-waged partner and

two children needs an income of €578 per week to have a minimum essential standard of living. Reducing the minimum wage by 1 euro per hour would see this weekly income fall to just €298, or 51 per cent of this basic threshold of decency.

If earnings in Ireland have to be reduced, it makes far more economic – as well as moral – sense to start at the top. A cut of €100,000 will not affect the real purchasing power of someone with an annual salary of €1 million. A cut of €10 a week will seriously affect the purchasing power of someone on €300 a week. All the evidence suggests that the effect of greater income inequality would be to raise the already problematic saving rate – the rich don't have to spend; ordinary workers do.

The public understands this very well. Attacks on the minimum wage are given great play in the media, but they do not have public support. In the Tasc/Behaviour and Attitudes survey, 16 per cent of people supported an *increase* in the minimum wage, 29 per cent supported the setting of a *maximum* wage, and 49 per cent supported a combination of both measures.

Developing a more equal society is about much more than wealth or income, of course. Income disparities – up to a point – would certainly matter less in a society that could guarantee basic decencies to all its citizens. But wealth and income cannot be ignored. Large disparities of wealth both reflect and perpetuate disparities of power that are incompatible with the existence of a meaningful republic.

Without a full-scale reordering of society – which is unlikely to happen in an Ireland that finds even minimal political change virtually unthinkable – two immediate steps can be taken. Neither is particularly radical but, taken together and in tandem with the changes suggested elsewhere in this book, they could make a very significant contribution towards the creation of a more equal society.

The first is that idea of a maximum wage. There is a strong case for having an effective ceiling of, say, €100,000, at least for an emergency period of three years. This could be imposed directly in the public sector (including the banks, which are effectively public companies) and through taxation measures in the private sector. Such a measure might, however, create genuine difficulties for some transnational corporations, who need to attract already highly paid workers from abroad. A more effective system, therefore, might be one in which, within each public or private enterprise, the highest paid workers would be paid at most a fixed multiple of the earnings of the lowest paid. If the multiple were five, for example, the most a chief executive who employed someone at a rate of €20,000 a year could earn would be €100,000. If bosses wanted to increase their own salaries, they would have to tackle low pay in their companies.

The second means of reducing income inequality is the obvious one: create a fair tax system. Ireland faces a double challenge with taxation. It has to find a way to raise more revenue in a manner that is sustainable and can replace the 17 per cent of the government's income that was coming from property-related taxes (stamp duty, VAT on building materials, income tax on builders' wages) at the height of the boom. And it has to create something whose absence has always weakened the idea of a republic – a tax system that is trusted to be fair. There is a dirty legacy of impunity for organised tax evasion, tax shelters for the rich and amnesties for tax dodgers to be overcome.

During the Celtic Tiger years, there was a myth that 'we'

were all rich. This has been replaced by a new myth – that 'we' are all poor. This is nonsense. The crash undoubtedly took a heavy toll on household wealth, through the collapse in the value of property assets and the disastrous perform- ance of pension funds. There have certainly been high-profile casualties among the super-rich, principally among the prop- erty developers (though many continue to enjoy a lifestyle that is far more opulent than anything available to those who are paying for their lost gambles). But the huge amount of wealth transferred from ordinary mortgage holders to land- owners during the long property boom hasn't simply evapo- rated. For everyone who lost money by buying overpriced land and property, someone made money by selling it.

There is a startling counter-intuitive fact that was given very little coverage in the Irish media. Ireland's 'high net worth' population *rose* by over 10 per cent in 2009, with an additional 1,800 Irish people becoming 'high net worth in- dividuals' (HNWIs). According to the annual World Wealth Report, published by Merrill Lynch Global Wealth Manage- ment and Capgemini, in 2009 there were 18,100 HNWIs in Ireland, defined as having investable assets of $1 million or more, bringing the total up from 16,300 in 2008. Also in 2009 a further eighteen Irish 'ultra-HNWIs', defined as hav- ing investable assets of $30 million or more, were created, bringing the total up to 181.

In the 1980s and early 1990s, the last time Ireland was 'broke' and the public finances were in disarray, there was ac- tually plenty of money floating around. It was, however, suc- cessfully kept out of the sight of the Revenue in 'bogus non- resident accounts' and schemes like the Ansbacher scam. The Central Bank and the Department of Finance decided not to know what they knew about this process. This allowed the crisis in the public finances to be defined entirely from one end – what the state was spending rather than what it was taking in through taxes. There is a strong instinct in the new crisis to repeat this process – albeit more subtly and with less flagrant illegality. The fiscal crisis is to be understood as being entirely about spending and not at all about tax.

Yet the evidence suggests that many people are still well off. Expensive fee-paying private schools continue to thrive: in April 2010 there were 26,000 pupils in fee-paying schools, which charge fees of up to €6,000 per year, or €16,000 a year for boarding schools. These schools have a fee income of €100 million a year between them.[10] Indeed, such was the demand for places that ten private schools in Dublin could substantially increase their fees for the 2010–11 school year, reflecting 'strong demand by parents for private education which has been largely unaffected by the economic downturn'.[11]

There were 7,018 new private cars licensed in July 2010, compared with 4,355 in July 2009, an increase of 61.1 per cent. Overall new car sales were up 50 per cent at over 79,000 to the end of August. The most popular new car? The luxury BMW Series 5, with models starting at a mere €41,750. In August alone, 350 of these BMWs were sold in Ireland.

And the amount of savings held by Irish people has dramatically increased – there has been what the Central Bank calls 'a large jump in precautionary savings'. The irony, indeed, is that while the government is borrowing large sums abroad, the savings of Irish people are being lent out to foreign banks. NCB stockbrokers pointed out in July 2010 that 'the huge increase in the private sector savings rate is offsetting the large amount of government borrowing so that Ireland will actually be a net lender to the world'.

But although there is enough money in Ireland to support

a modest but decent republic, with a fair tax system to re-distribute that money, moves towards even the most basic equity have been timid. Changes were introduced in the 2006 and 2007 Finance Acts to ensure that anyone earning over €500,000 would pay at least 20 per cent tax – hardly a radical step, considering that workers on relatively modest incomes move on to a top rate of 42 per cent.

These changes did yield some results – an extra €40 million or so a year was raised. Yet the effect of the changes remains extremely modest. In a Revenue study, 189 individuals with a declared income of over €500,000 paid tax at an average effective rate of just 19.86 per cent. Meanwhile, 234 high-income individuals with declared incomes of between €250,000 and €500,000 enjoyed an average effective tax rate of just 13.82 per cent.[12] There were still fifty-four individuals with incomes up to €500,000 who paid tax at less than 5 per cent, and 143 who paid tax at less than 15 per cent.

It should be noted that the declared income figures that are used by the Revenue refer to income *after* deductions for pension contributions, personal tax credits, capital allowances for plant and machinery and business-related losses. It is likely that the real before-tax incomes of these individuals are much higher.

A little further down the income ladder, about 3,800 people who earned more than €100,000 in 2009 paid no tax at all on their income. Unsurprisingly, the majority of these people were company directors.[13] Top earners in Ireland are in fact very lightly taxed. Just 29 per cent of the gross household income of the 10 per cent of households with the highest incomes goes on tax and social insurance contributions.

We have to face up to the fact that Ireland has been significantly under-taxed. The income from the property bubble

– and to a lesser extent from the unstable international financial services sector – allowed Fianna Fáil-led governments to do what they like to do best: avoid hard choices. Social spending could increase while taxes were reduced – the magic circle that every government dreams of. The tax burden in Ireland (measured as a percentage of GNP) was the seventeenth lowest in the EU, with most of the lower countries being in the former Eastern European bloc. If GDP is used as the benchmark – and in this case, there is an argument for doing so, since the multinationals do pay tax here – Ireland has the fifth lowest taxes in the EU, with only Latvia, Lithuania, Slovakia and Romania behind it.[14] In order to fund the high-quality universal public services which are essential to economic equality, Ireland's overall tax take needs to rise gradually from a low base of 35 per cent of GDP (in 2008) to a European average of 45 per cent of GDP.

This is not as drastic as it seems. Few people in Ireland really believed they were overtaxed in the year 2000, yet effective tax rates (total tax paid as a proportion of gross income) were significantly higher then than they are now. In 2000 a dual-income couple earning €100,000 had an effective tax rate of 36 per cent. They now have an effective tax rate of 28 per cent. For middle-income earners, a return to the taxation levels that were the norm before the 'low tax, light regulation' ideology took hold does not constitute cruel and unusual punishment. This is especially so in the context of the proposals here to guarantee essential public services.

Nor, contrary to the dire warnings of those with a vested interest in low taxation, is an increased tax take a threat to international competiveness. Social Justice Ireland has pointed out that of all the countries ranked above Ireland in the Global Competitiveness Index for which comparable figures are available, just one, the US, does not have a significantly higher tax take. Investment in infrastructure, education and innovation are of far more consequence to competitiveness than overall taxation levels. If Ireland were taxed as heavily as Sweden, it would have an extra €18 billion to spend on them.

But it is crucial, both economically and for social cohesion, that the burden of increased taxes does not fall on the middle-income earners alone. If ordinary people are to buy in to the necessity for higher taxes, they need to believe two things – that the system is fair and that the wealthy are paying their proper share.

One way to make the system fairer is to stamp down harder on tax evasion and the under-declaration of income, which the C&AG has estimated at an average of 30 per cent. There are plenty of people with high-level financial skills who have lost their jobs. Bring in, say, 500 of them, on two-year contracts initially, to conduct audits of tax declarations. The logic is simple. Many people with extra income under-declare their earnings on self-assessment forms. We know this because in 2009 a mere 12,400 audits were done and yielded tax of almost €600 million. That's nearly €50,000 per audit. More officials carrying out more audits would easily pay for themselves, would raise extra revenue and would encourage greater honesty in the declaration of incomes.

There also needs to be an enhancement both of the Revenue's resources for investigations and of the legal penalties for tax evasion. As of April 2010, special Revenue investigations in the wake of tribunals of inquiry, the DIRT inquiry and other scandals had yielded €2.6 billion in tax from 34,300 individuals. But there were just six successful prosecutions for serious tax evasion in 2009, with twelve further cases due to come before the courts. The total number of convictions for all Revenue offences, 2,144, resulted in a total of just €5.3 million in fines. There have to be serious mandatory penalties for tax evasion and Revenue has to be given the resources to investigate and bring cases to the courts.

The next step is to clean up the jungle of tax reliefs in which incomes can be lawfully hidden. The Commission on Taxation identified, for the first time on the public record, no fewer than 115 'tax expenditures'. These tax breaks are not free – someone else pays for them. As the Commission puts it, 'Tax expenditure necessarily involves the imposition of a corresponding financial burden on others as a result of the tax forgone through the tax expenditure . . . Tax expenditures are equivalent to direct public spending and, as such, they should be reviewed as regularly and as carefully.'

Yet, farcically, the cost of many of these reliefs is unknown: 'throughout our review we encountered many instances where basic cost and benefit data were not available for tax expenditures. Where costs were available, we note that the quality of these estimates was variable . . . It is difficult to see how accountability and control in the allocation of public resources can be adequately secured where basic information on the annual cost of so many tax expenditures remains unavailable or unreliable.'

Broadly, the Commission recommended that tax reliefs be scrapped and that, if a certain goal is deemed worthy of public spending, the government should pay for it directly. At the very least, each tax break should automatically expire at the end of every financial year, unless it is specifically renewed following a proper cost–benefit analysis.

Tasc estimates that tax breaks cost the state approximately €7.4 billion in 2009. If tax breaks on personal income tax and corporation tax were simply reduced to EU average levels, they would cost just €2.2 billion, a difference of €5.2 billion. As well as raising over €5 billion in revenue, this single measure would have a very significant effect on inequality, since the vast bulk of the saving would come from higher income earners (the OECD notes that these breaks 'benefit the highest earners the most') and could be redistributed in the form of better services to the society as a whole.

As well as restoring the tax burden for middle-income earners to the levels of 2000 and cutting €5 billion from tax breaks, there should be a new third tax rate of 48 per cent for those earning over €100,000. More importantly, however, there has to be a shift towards sustainable taxation that can fund proper local government. This has to involve the adoption of something that is entirely normal in the rest of the developed world – property taxes.

Ireland has had a bad habit of scrapping taxes on property: slashing capital gains tax on property dealings, allowing huge transfers of land as gifts or through inheritance without tax, abolishing 'imputed rental' income tax, abolishing domestic rates, abolishing residential property tax and farm tax. This is in spite of the fact that, as the Commission on Taxation put it, 'annual or recurrent taxes on immoveable property are a common feature of tax systems in most industrialised and developed countries'.

During the boom years – especially those of the property mania – it was possible to do without property tax because stamp duty from the sale of houses was producing so much revenue – €1.3 billion in 2006 and €1.1 billion 2007. And stamp duty was just one of the sources of revenue from the property boom – overall, property-related tax revenues jumped by almost €7 billion between 2001 and 2006.

That money is gone and should stay gone – it is madness for a government to depend on revenue from a source as unstable and unpredictable as house sales, not least because it gives governments a vested interest in inflating the property market. It is time to get rid of stamp duty and replace it with a more stable and equitable property tax.

Property taxes are even more attractive now than they were in the past. In an era of globalisation, they are immune to mobility. In a culture of clever tax avoidance, they are hard to get out of – a house is not easy to hide. And in a period of economic austerity, property taxes do not depress the economy. As the Commission puts it: '[Property] tax does not directly affect the decision to supply or demand labour. The tax base is stable and tax revenue from this source is predictable, and the tax base is immobile, and is therefore less likely to distort economic behaviour.' If anything, property taxes should encourage investors away from unproductive investment in bricks and mortar and towards more productive sectors of the economy.

A property tax of 1 per cent could raise €4 billion a year.[15] In fairness to those who have paid stamp duty in the last few years, they should be given a 'holiday' from property tax for, say, five years. Equally, those on low incomes should be exempt.

People will always complain about taxes, but a proper tax system is essential to a republic. We know from bitter experience that a low tax regime did not create either a decent society or a sustainable economy. If citizens can see that their taxes are creating a society to be proud of and that everyone is contributing a fair share, we might even get to the point where proposals to cut taxes are seen, not as a promise, but as a threat.

5

Ethical Austerity:
The Decency of Citizenship

The great historian of postwar Europe, the late Tony Judt, recalled that he had grown up in England after the Second World War when there was a single word for the way most people lived: austerity. The word has a chill to it, summoning to the mind images of bony-faced medieval monks with wasted bodies and a fanatical coldness in their faraway gaze. And austerity is where we live now. After the ball, we are back among the ashes and cinders.

But if we're going to have austerity, we should decide what it means. For those who are still in charge, its meaning is clear – it is something that is good for other people. It is the new version of what poverty used to be for the Church: a virtuous blessing that was best bestowed on unimportant people. Austerity has been reduced to 'austerity measures' – cutting welfare payments and public services – that apply only in the mildest way to those who impose and support them.

Yet there is another meaning of austerity, what Judt called 'the virtues of the bare-bones age': 'No one would welcome its return. But austerity was not just an economic condition: it aspired to be a public ethic.' At its core was a notion of 'moral seriousness in public life . . . a coherence of intention and action, an ethic of political responsibility.' Judt mourned the fact that 'We have substituted endless commerce for public purpose, and expect no higher aspirations from our leaders.' Austerity, he suggested, should be imagined as the opposite, not of prosperity, but of wasteful luxury: 'If we want better rulers, we must learn to ask more from them and less for ourselves. A little austerity might be in order.'[1]

These notions of public virtue have been deeply embedded in the history of republicanism and have given that ideal much of its strength as well as its cant, hypocrisy and fanaticism. But they have a renewed meaning in the twenty-first century. The relentless appetite for more stuff has created a culture of consumption that will end up consuming our societies, our environments, perhaps our very existence. We have reached the limits, both physical and moral, of that culture. A good dose of genuine austerity would do us no harm – if we understand austerity as 'the virtues of a bare-bones age'. Instead of thinking about austerity as a harsh laxative to be delivered to others, we can think of it as an opportunity to cut out what is wasteful, excessive and superfluous, and to concentrate on what matters.

It is certainly true in Ireland that we have no great choice but to adopt austerity. Equally, though, we have a very specific need for it, one that is largely unrelated to the economic collapse. If we think of austerity as a 'public ethic', it can begin to fill the hole that is left where a different kind of ethical system used to be. Morality in Ireland was outsourced to the Church, which defined it for the most part around issues of sexuality and reproduction and paid little attention to public or commercial ethics. Irish people accepted the Church's notion that what happened in the bedroom was of much more moral concern than what happened in the boardroom.

For example, the Irish report of the European Value Systems Study in 1984 shows that the Irish believed that

homosexuality, divorce, prostitution or having an affair
were significantly worse sins than cheating on your taxes.
Asked to rank certain conduct between one and ten, with one
the most unjustifiable, Irish respondents rated prostitution
a 2.1, homosexuality a 2.7, divorce a 3.2 and cheating on
taxes a 3.6.[2] On this tolerance of tax evasion the Irish came
'top of the European league'. This was a reflection of the
weight given to different moral issues in the preaching of the
Church – sex was more important than money, the private
realm than the public realm.

This system was always tempered by the hypocrisy which
may be its most enduring legacy, but its collapse – and the
failure to replace it with a civic or public ethic – was one of
the reasons for the fatal triumph of consumerism in the boom
years. There was a void to be filled and no shortage of shiny
stuff to fill it with. Ireland doesn't need to go into penitential
mode and engage in collective self-flagellation to expunge its
sins of self-indulgence and self-delusion. But it does need to
develop a republican ethic of citizenship in which excess is
not worshipped, rules are agreed to and kept and responsibility is taken – for ourselves and our society. Part of the
challenge is that this ethic has to be one for a post-theocratic
state, one that is hospitable to, and can attract the allegiance
of, people of all faiths and none.

Much of this sounds abstract, and there is a danger of laps-
ing into vapid pieties, so let's start with something concrete:
rules. Everyone knows by now that 'regulation' – or rather
its absence – is at the core of the collapse of the Irish banking
system. Why has Ireland been so bad at regulating itself, especially in relation to the conduct of business? There are big,
cultural answers to this question, to do with the very limited
ideas of morality that the Church transmitted, or with the

corrupting influence of the powerlessness that comes with colonialism. But there is also a simpler, blunter answer: rules are subverted because it suits some people to do so and because they have the ear of those who are supposed to enforce the rules.

Let's take a single case in point: the role of auditors and non-executive directors in the banking crash. Many decent, ethical people work as auditors, and many highly distinguished people were on the boards of banks, but collectively they ended up being complicit in the recklessness and irresponsibility of the banks. Some of the world's most prestigious firms of auditors pored over the books of the banks every year: KPMG for Allied Irish and Irish Nationwide; PwC for Bank of Ireland; Ernst and Young for Anglo Irish. Their skills were highly valued. In the last year of the boom, 2007, AIB paid KPMG €7 million and Irish Nationwide paid them €224,000. Bank of Ireland paid PwC €12.5 million; Anglo Irish paid Ernst & Young €1.8 million.

There is no reason to think that any of the highly trained people who carried out this work were less than professional, diligent and well-intentioned. Yet not one of these firms ever reported any problem with any of the banks. Even the extraordinary shenanigans at Anglo – money moved onto the balance sheet just in time for the annual accounts, then sent back to where it came from; massive loans to directors – failed to attract any comment in the accounts. And there is no evidence that any executive director asked the kind of questions that would force any of these issues into the open.

How could this happen? What kind of ethical culture facilitates such collective silence? Two factors made it possible – political cowardice and personal intimidation. For any system of ethical rules to work, governments have to be willing to enforce them against the inevitable objections of those who have a vested interest in laxity. And, perhaps even more importantly, individuals with a conscience have to be able to speak up knowing that they will be listened to and supported. Neither of these conditions has been present in Ireland.

The political cowardice can be illustrated in the story of one piece of legislation. In 1999, when the Public Accounts Committee reported on the DIRT scandal, it raised exactly the questions everybody asked again in the wake of the banking collapse in 2008 – where were the auditors? Part of what came out of all of this were the ideas, put into law in 2004, that banks and their internal auditors would have to make compliance statements to the financial regulator in order to create 'a culture of compliance by developing a greater sense of accountability and responsibility among company directors and by developing good systems of internal controls within companies so that directors could commit themselves to compliance in good faith'. What happened to this rather mild provision is typical of the invertebrate nature of political ethics.

Firstly, instead of saying that banks would have to make compliance statements to the financial regulator (FR), the legislation introduced by Fianna Fáil and the Progressive Democrats put things the other way round – the financial regulator could ask for a statement. As the new governor of the Central Bank, Patrick Honohan, puts it in his report on the banking crisis, 'it was not a requirement on a financial services provider to make an annual compliance statement; rather, it provided the FR with a discretionary power to seek such a statement'.[3] A straightforward proposition – banks have to declare that they are complying with the rules – is twisted here into a slithery suggestion that the regulator may (or may not) ask a bank to say that it is complying with the rules. This doesn't happen by accident; crafting this kind of language is an art form.

So what happens next? Does the regulator look for compliance statements from the banks? Well, not exactly. The Financial Services Regulatory Authority decides, in November 2004, to prepare and publish a public consultation paper on the issue. And then it decides not to issue a public consultation paper, but rather to 'conduct an informal pre-consultation process . . . among selected participants'.

And who are the 'selected participants'? The banks, of course. The FR has cosy chats with its own industry and consumer panels, with the chairman of Allied Irish Bank, and with five financial industry lobby groups: Financial Services Ireland, the Irish Insurance Federation, the Professional Insurance Brokers Association, the Irish Brokers Association and the Irish Association of Investment Managers. Out of these 'pre-consultation' consultations it emerges that 'the resistance to this proposal [to ask for compliance statements] from industry was very strong'.

And then the industry lobbyists go to where the power is – to the Minister for Finance, Brian Cowen, and his officials. Suddenly, the financial regulator reports to his board that

> the Department of Finance, following contacts with industry bodies regarding their concerns, requested that the Financial Regulator not proceed with the consultation process on the implementation of this requirement without engaging in further discussion with the Department. The Authority was also informed in December 2006 that the Minister for Finance felt that it was important to assess the competitiveness issue.

The 'competiveness issue' is familiar code – if we impose any ethical obligations on banks, it might frighten away some of those we are trying to attract to our own Bermuda on the Liffey, the Financial Services Centre in Dublin. The word has come down from Cowen – go easy on this one, lest we frighten the nervous thoroughbreds. And so, the financial regulator goes back to talk to the Department of Finance. And 'following a discussion with the Department of Finance it was agreed by the FR not to implement the provision as set out in the Central Bank Act, 1997' because 'the implementation of the provision would damage competitiveness; and the application of the provision was not consistent with a principles based approach' (as opposed, that is to a rules-based approach) to regulation. A very timid attempt to create some kind of formal ethical obligation for bank directors is rudely ditched – whatever the law passed by the Dáil might say.

Patrick Honohan remarks of this sorry episode that it 'illustrate(s) how an important FR initiative to codify its principles in one respect ran into the sand as the organisation deferred to industry pressure'. But this is so diplomatic it borders on the disingenuous. The 'industry pressure' proves decisive because it gets the backing of the person who is supposed to be looking out for the public interest – the minister, Brian Cowen. It is the job of ministers to implement the law and to stand up to lobby groups. In our political culture, there is no guarantee that that job will be done.

This small episode crystallises a number of questions about what needs to be done if a public ethic is to be established in practice. First, though, we need to look at the other side of the equation. What happens to moral people within organisations? Ultimately, no system of rules will work if there are too few people who find it hard to look at themselves in the mirror when they have seen wrongdoing and looked the other way.

Again, let's take a single episode from the world of banking. In 2004, in what ought to have been a public warning that the ethical culture of Irish banking had not improved since the DIRT inquiry, Allied Irish Bank confessed – after an investigation by RTE – that it had overcharged its customers by €34 million. Two years later, it owned up to a further €32 million. But two years before the first revelation, in 2002, the bank's head of internal audit, Eugene McErlean, had uncovered the overcharging. Looking at the fees levied by branches across the state, he made a rough calculation that the bank may have wrongly taken up to €75 million of customers' money.

McErlean had no intention of becoming a whistleblower. He simply did what he was supposed to do. 'I was just doing my job as an auditor. There was no big deal. I was obliged to report my findings both to the bank and to the Financial Regulator.'[4] Instead of being congratulated for doing his job properly, however, McErlean was fired by AIB. His departure was announced at the same time as the bank revealed a huge fraud in its subsidiary in Maryland, giving the false impression that the two events were somehow connected. Equally, when the overcharging scandal eventually became public in 2004, the bank blamed its 'internal control procedures', hinting that McErlean, the very person who had discovered and tried to deal with the problem, was responsible for it.

McErlean got no help from the Financial Regulator. When he initially reported his findings, the regulator seemed to be taking them very seriously. When he returned for a second meeting, however, he was, he says, curtly told that he should withdraw his allegations. (Officials from the office of the Financial Regulator denied in 2009 that this had happened.) Having signed a confidentiality agreement with the bank, McErlean was effectively silenced, and the regulator did nothing until the scandal was uncovered as a result of information from a different source in 2004.

This is, in many ways, a typical tale of corporate cynicism and regulatory spinelessness. But there are two distinctive and instructive aspects to the story. The first is that McErlean was the third person to hold the job of head of internal audit at AIB since the post was established in 1990. The first, Tony Spollen, came across the DIRT scam, reported it to the board and was fired for his trouble. The second, Ian Howley, discovered something that made him uneasy and was 'moved' to another job. In other words, the largest bank in the country had a systematic policy of punishing auditors for doing their job properly. McErlean's fate wasn't a one-off incident, it was a result of corporate omerta. The stool pigeons got whacked. And nobody did anything about it. No one at the top of AIB ever suffered any consequences for the enforcement of this policy.

The second telling aspect of the story is that the lack of protection for a man like McErlean who naively believed that doing his job meant telling the truth is not accidental. It is not, like so much in Irish law, a matter of mere neglect or accidental omission. It is the way it is meant to be.

In 2007 Brian Cowen asked the Company Law Review Group (CLRG), the statutory body that recommends changes in Irish company law, to consider the inclusion of a provision to protect whistleblowers in the forthcoming Companies Consolidation and Reform Bill. There were strong submissions in favour of such a provision from the Office of the Director of Corporate Enforcement and the Irish Congress of

Trade Unions. They counted for nothing. The review group completely rejected the idea of whistleblower protection.

Its reasoning is a reminder of the reasons why political satire is almost impossible in Ireland. In considering the question, the CLRG claimed that 'any proposed changes to the law must seek to balance corporate governance and commercial probity with the wider promotion of enterprise and the facilitation of commerce'. This in itself is a highly revealing statement. It makes the assumption that 'corporate governance and commercial probity' are opposing values to 'enterprise and the facilitation of commerce'. What hope could there be of ethical reform from those who do not understand that probity is not something to be balanced against successful and sustainable commerce, or that the basis of all long-term commercial success is trust based on honesty?

Given such assumptions, it is perhaps not so surprising that the group (made up of lawyers, accountants, bankers and others of the great and good) came up with one of the finest declarations of peace in our time since Neville Chamberlain got off the plane from Munich: 'One cannot say that there is any evidence of endemic failure in relation to corporate governance or its enforcement in Ireland that negatively affects the investment climate and which requires enhanced "whistleblowing" provisions.'

And if whistleblowers were encouraged, they might reveal things which would give foreigners a bad impression of dear old Ireland: 'There is risk of negative connotations attaching internationally to the heretofore positively perceived Irish business sector and to the reputation of companies. In such circumstances, there is a knock-on impact for employees, their jobs and a focus on "wrongdoing" within the company. Given the fact that no analogous provisions exist in other EU countries, Irish companies could gain a reputation, mischievously, for having an underlying disregard for good corporate governance practice, which is patently not the case. Ireland's reputation as a lightly regulated economy could suffer.'[5]

It might be suggested that 'that was then' and that, in the light of the disastrous consequences of bad corporate governance since 2007, even the smug Irish Establishment could not think this way now. But the smugness was every bit as idiotic in 2007 as it seems now. No one had to wait for the banking collapse to reveal 'evidence of endemic failure in relation to corporate governance or its enforcement in Ireland'. It was already amply documented in the tribunal of inquiry into the beef processing industry, in the DIRT inquiry, in the Ansbacher report and many other places. If the finest minds in the field of company law had paid so little attention to all of these scandals in 2007, why should we imagine that they have learned much from the banking crisis of 2008?

If there is a real issue of 'competitiveness' it is that the prevalence of fraud constitutes a competitive disadvantage for Irish firms. Half of Irish companies have confirmed that they have experienced a significant instance of fraud in the past two years, compared to 16 per cent of companies globally and 21 per cent in Western Europe as a whole. Seventy per cent of Irish businesses (compared to 28 per cent globally) have been asked by their boards to provide details of any internal investigations into fraud, bribery or corrupt practices in the last twelve months. Eighty-five per cent of Irish businesses report that their board members are increasingly concerned about their own personal liability in terms of fraud, bribery and corruption (in comparison to 76 per cent globally).[6] Fraud and deception are serious threats to Irish companies – more so than to their international competitors.

And yet attempts to enforce a public ethic of honest dealing remain extraordinarily weak. Consider one of the basic financial sins – insider trading. When someone uses inside knowledge to buy or sell shares at the right time, others dealing in those shares are cheated. In theory, insider trading is banned in Ireland. In practice, it has become effectively impossible to accuse anyone of engaging in the practice.

A high-profile case of alleged insider trading is that of Jim Flavin, head of the large holding group DCC, who, having previously seen Fyffes internal trading accounts, sold shares of the fruit importer shortly before they took a drastic fall on the stock market. Fyffes sued Flavin and won in the Supreme Court, getting €42 million back from Flavin, who always vehemently denied that he had engaged in insider trading.

What matters about this case is that the High Court subsequently appointed an inspector, Bill Shipsey, to investigate the affair. Shipsey exonerated Flavin of wrongdoing because 'I have concluded that Mr Flavin genuinely believed that he was not in possession of price-sensitive information.' This belief, based on his consultations with colleagues and advisers was, in Shipsey's view as well as that of the Supreme Court, actually wrong. But what matters is not objective fact but the state of mind of the person engaged in a transaction. Since both Jim Flavin's business peers and his legal and tax advisers believed (wrongly) that the transaction was okay, no legal action can be taken against him. Breaches of company law that would result in serious criminal sanctions in other countries are okay in Ireland so long as they fall within the Irish definitions of 'genuine belief'.

The circle is neatly vicious: low ethical standards lead people to believe they're acting properly, which means they're not breaking the law, which means the low standards are fine.

This seems to extend even to basic practices like the keeping of minutes of board meetings. When DCC transferred its Fyffes shares to a Dutch holding company, the minutes recorded the move as 'corporate restructuring'. This was a straightforward lie. The entire purpose was to avoid capital gains tax on the sale of the shares. But the Shipsey report is sympathetic to this practice: '"Corporate restructuring" was an understandable euphemism for the tax scheme. DCC would not have wanted the minutes to record what was, in fact, the express purpose of the scheme.'

Even after the crash, it remains extremely hard to establish in Ireland notions of right and wrong behaviour that are taken for granted elsewhere. Insider trading is still a matter of what you sincerely believe you're doing, rather than of objective rules. Using 'euphemisms' to disguise tax avoidance schemes in company minutes is still 'understandable'. The desire to believe that there is no systemic problem with corporate governance in Ireland and that anyone who says otherwise is letting us down in front of the foreigners is still deeply embedded within the mentality of the governing elite. People like Eugene McErlean, who think that 'doing my job' means telling the truth, are still firmly on the outside, banished for being dangerously naive. People who never use the phrase 'doing my job' without putting the word 'only' before it are still on the inside, keeping quiet.

What do we do about this? If we pull at the threads of the 'compliance statements' and McErlean stories, certain necessities become obvious.

We have to curb the excessive influence of lobby groups of the kind that could cause a minister for finance to lean on a banking regulator to overturn a provision enacted by the Dáil. Ireland is highly unusual in the developed world in having no formal or statutory system for regulating or registering lobbyists. A government statement of December 2000 indicated that 'it is the Government's intention to introduce a regulation and registration system for those who operate on a paid basis as lobbyists in one form or another seeking to exert influence on political and public service decision making'. The intention never came to fruition – perhaps the lobbyists successfully lobbied against it. A Labour Party private members' 'Registration of Lobbyists Bill, 2003' was voted down by the government. It would have established a register of lobbyists, made it compulsory to register their activities with the Standards in Public Office Commission, set out a code of conduct, made it illegal for sitting politicians to engage in lobbying and banned holders of office or their advisers from acting as lobbyists for two years after leaving office. This was not the first time a Labour bill to this broad effect was voted down. It happened on five occasions: twice in 1999, then again in 2000, 2003 and 2008, each time bringing promises from government to enact its own legislation. In July 2010 the environment minister John Gormley again promised legislation.

But while registering lobbyists is one thing, actually limiting undue influence is another. The best formal way to do this is through transparency in the operation of government. It is crucial that the Freedom of Information Act is restored to what it was before Charlie McCreevy vandalised it. But in relation to lobbying, retrospective information is not enough. All government departments should publish, on a weekly basis, details of who the minister or senior officials met and what was discussed. The same should apply to all public bodies (including the Central Bank). If a proposal or issue is being discussed with any one interest group, the views of all other stakeholders should be actively invited. Legitimate lobbying has nothing to hide – people with a stake in a policy decision have a right to be heard. What matters, though, is that *all* people with a stake in a decision get to be heard.

No change in lobbying will matter unless there's a commensurate change in the mentality on the other side of the table. Ethics legislation has to be strengthened, especially in relation to sanctions for breaches of the rules. Essentially, politicians found to have acted unethically face suspension from the Dáil or Seanad for twenty sitting days. This is far too weak. A detailed proposal for a much stronger set of sanctions was in fact made by the Fianna Fáil/Progressive Democrats government in 2002. The then chief whip, Mary Hanafin, 'announced details of the powers of the new Corruption Assets Bureau which was promised by the Taoiseach in his Fianna Fáil Ard Fheis speech earlier this year'. It was impressive stuff. The bureau would be 'a statutory body specifically dedicated to tracing and recovering the proceeds of corruption'. Not only would any corruptly acquired wealth be seized, but the value would be calculated in present-day terms, so that 'if a person corruptly received £1,000 in 1960 and bought a house with that money the High Court will be entitled to order that the current day value of the house be frozen or forfeited'. Even better news was that 'the proceeds of corruption obtained through the Corruption Assets Bureau will be held for the benefit of the Irish people. In this way we will restore the benefits wrongly taken from the Irish people through corruption of those engaged in public service or holding elected office.' But sadly, the Corruption Assets Bureau slipped the government's mind. Perhaps there was not enough evidence of dodgy dealing to justify its establishment.

As well as strengthening sanctions, a new Ethics Act needs

to set a single, comprehensive and comprehensible set of rules for what is and is not acceptable behaviour for all holders of public office, in national or local government or in public bodies. The confusion in the current situation has been pointed out by the Standards in Public Office Commission (SIPO), which is supposed to police the rules:

> since the enactment of the Ethics in Public Office Act 1995, legislation has been introduced to provide separate rules for the disclosure of interests in over fifty public bodies. The intention of the Ethics Acts is to provide a clear and comprehensive framework for the disclosure of interests by public officials. This is not served by the enactment of legislation applying to some but not all public bodies which overlaps with the provisions of the Ethics Acts. The implication may be that the Oireachtas considers the provisions of the Ethics Acts to be inadequate if they must be supplemented by separate legislation in certain public bodies. In addition, there is considerable scope for confusion on the part of persons who are obliged to comply with separate disclosure provisions. There is also the possibility that a person may be found to have contravened the provisions of the Ethics Acts, but to have complied with other statutory disclosure provisions arising from the same circumstance.[7]

More importantly, the current legislation is very weak in the way it defines 'connected' for the purposes of deciding whether or not an office holder has to declare an interest. You don't have to declare yourself 'connected' to a company unless you have effective control of it. The absurdity of this rule became evident when a complaint was made under the

act that Seán FitzPatrick and Lar Bradshaw, who were directors both of Anglo Irish Bank and of the Dublin Docklands
Development Authority, which was engaging in disastrous
dealings with Anglo, had not declared a conflict of interest.
SIPO felt it had to dismiss the complaint because 'While it
may be that both held substantial shareholdings in the bank,
the decision rested on the fact that there was no evidence that
either held "control" of the bank.' There could be no better
proof that the current ethics regime is close to useless and
that a far more robust one needs to be put in place.

The link between money and politics has to be completely
severed. The political parties have been given ample opportunity to show that they can operate responsibly a system
in which they get funding both from the taxpayer and from
private donations. They have abused that privilege with flagrant cynicism.

The Electoral Act of 1997, which was supposed to clean
up political funding, always looked deeply flawed but has
proved to be farcical. The Act delivered a lot of public money
to the main political parties: €13.6 million in 2009. In return,
it limited donations to parties to €6,308 and required that
donations over €5,078.95 be disclosed. The parties took the
public money and then cynically evaded the requirements for
disclosure. There are clearly an awful lot of citizens or corporations who feel patriotically inspired to donate €5,078.94
to Fianna Fáil or Fine Gael – perhaps a cent more, but not
two cents. We know this because the parties have managed
to declare fewer and fewer donations each year. In 2008 the
three biggest parties declared a grand total of €96,000 between them – the lowest up to that point. But in 2009 they
played one of those card games where the object is to lose
every hand. They emerged triumphant with a great gaping

zero. Fianna Fáil, Fine Gael and Labour got not a single pub-
lically disclosable donation between them in 2009. What
makes this even more remarkable is that 2009 was a busy
election year, with European and local elections and two Dáil
by-elections.

The system is even worse than this makes it sound. Below
a threshold of €126.97, a donation can be given anonymously and does not need to be registered at all by the politician
who receives it. He or she does not have to put the money in
a special political account – it can be simply trousered. This
may seem like a very small amount, but as SIPO points out,
'large donations could be split into amounts below €126.97
to avoid the registration and disclosure requirement'. A company, if it could organise things quietly enough, could make
an entirely anonymous, unregistered and untraceable donation of €125,000 to a politician by getting a thousand employees to each send €125 in cash.

What is especially outrageous is that parties, even though
they receive substantial public funding, have no obligation
to keep, let alone publish, proper accounts. As SIPO notes,
'There is no requirement under the Electoral Acts for political parties to keep proper books and accounts, to specify all
donations received in these accounts or to make the accounts
public. It is not currently possible to know the annual income
of political parties nor to have a full picture of how elections
are funded . . . There is no requirement to furnish a full set of
income and expenditure statements, listing of debts and assets nor additional details as to how campaigns are funded.'
This is not true of any other group in the country. A small
theatre company that gets €50,000 a year from the Arts
Council has to provide its audited accounts. Yet the public
has a vital interest in knowing who's giving money to political

parties. It also has a right to know who parties owe money
to – large debts potentially impose large obligations. There
is no evidence, for example, that any party owed money to
Anglo Irish Bank, and the strong likelihood is that they did
not. But the public has no way of knowing such information
and therefore remains completely in the dark about whether
or not there may be conflicts of interest.

The necessary changes are obvious enough. All political
parties must be legally required to publish independently audited annual accounts. These accounts should also report on
income and expenditure of local branches. The loophole that
allows parties to declare as 'electoral spending' only money
spent after the election is actually called should be closed.
And private donations should effectively be banned. If it is
necessary for legal reasons to allow some level of contribution, it should be set at a very low level (say, €50 a year) and
should be disclosed. This does mean that it may be necessary
to increase the amount of money that parties get from the
state – current funds cannot be used to contest elections –
but this should be done with a frugality appropriate to the
times and with a refusal to fund unnecessary stunts. These
measures would certainly go some distance to changing a
culture in which the banking lobby may be confident of having the minister for finance on its side against the law and
the regulator.

In the end, however, even the highest ethical standards are
useless against cowardice, cynicism or laziness in office holders. The political culture itself has to change radically, not
least through an end to the tribal contest between two virtually identical centre-right populist parties. A genuine clash
of ideas and ideologies is necessary to give politics an edge.
Voters have to create that realignment for themselves.

These changes will address the implications of the first of our stories. But what of the second, the sacking of Eugene McErlean? Here we are looking at the need for a change in corporate culture based on the realisation that the opposition between successful enterprise on the one hand and probity on the other is not just wrong but fatal. Sustainable, long-term businesses are not built on having an eye for the main chance, covering up fraud and ineptitude and repeating the same crass mistakes over and over again.

In the legal field, we have to start by taking company law back from those who are currently framing it and who, on their own account, see their function as 'the wider promotion of enterprise and the facilitation of commerce'. There are plenty of agencies that exist to promote enterprise and commerce – this is not the role of the law. What the law should be there to do is to stop shysters destroying the long-term development of enterprise and commerce by refusing to accept that they have any ethical responsibilities.

A proper review of Irish company law could begin with asking: why is it that almost no one goes to jail for white-collar crime in Ireland? And then the next question: how can we can ensure that white-collar criminals no longer get away with it? It would ask what the law can do about the situation in which insider trading in Ireland is a matter of what you think you're doing and writing deliberately misleading company records is 'understandable'. It would set out to protect the decent majority in Irish business by rooting out those who see morality as a game of bluff.

This may be a wide-ranging process involving some difficult questions, such as whether we need to have special non-jury courts for complex fraud cases. But three immediate specifics would help to give a healthy shock to the system.

The first is a widening of the legal obligation on auditors to report suspected wrongdoing to outside authorities. Currently auditors have to report to the Director of Corporate Enforcement if they have 'reasonable grounds for believing that an indictable offence under the Companies Acts has been committed' – which is fine as far as it goes, but the grounds are actually very narrow. Recklessness of the kind engaged in by all of the banks does not constitute an indictable offence. Nor does the overcharging that Eugene McErlean discovered – the bank claimed that it was inadvertent. Even the massive collusion with tax fraud that was involved in the DIRT scandal does not necessarily come under this heading – no one in the banks was ever charged with an offence. And we have to assume that the auditors of Anglo Irish Bank did not form the opinion that any of the creative accounting that was going on there constituted a potentially indictable offence, since they did not report it. At the very least the definition of what auditors must report should be expanded to include reckless, unethical or dangerously incompetent conduct.

Secondly, the cronyism of Irish corporate culture needs to be smashed. Niall FitzGerald, the former Unilever chairman who came up through the 'claustrophobic' world of Irish business, remarked that part of the problem that led to Ireland's current crisis was 'that very intimacy, the knowledge that you can take one small envelope and write all the names that matter on the back of it. Because we're all human – you can think something very strongly, but to express to you, as a very good friend of mine, that I think you're screwing things up here and actually doing wrong things is quite tough.'[8]

This is not just an anecdotal perception. Multiple directorships create a dense network of cross-connections in the corporate world. Tasc's *Mapping the Golden Circle* report found that in the period 2005–7 a network of just thirty-nine people held positions in thirty-three of the forty top private companies and state-owned bodies. Between them, these thirty-nine held a total of ninety-three directorships. Of the forty private sector and state companies studied, just seven in all – and just two of them in the private sector – did not have at least one director who was not also a member of one of the other company's boards. Many of these directors also had directorships outside of the big forty companies. Between them, the highly connected thirty-nine held an astonishing 491 directorships. One individual was on no fewer than fifty-seven additional boards. The centre of this web was the banking system – the eleven most connected directors were all on the boards of at least one bank or building society each. But political connections were also evident – at least half of the most well-connected directors had sat as government appointees on the boards of state companies or held senior public service positions.

There are obvious ways to cut these connections. No one should be allowed to serve on the boards of more than three publicly quoted companies. And a new and independent system of appointment to state boards should be adopted, with people chosen by the Dáil for specified skills.

The third immediate change should be strong legislative protection for whistleblowers. This has been repeatedly called for by those who deal officially with corruption in both business and politics – the Office of the Director of Corporate Enforcement and the Standards in Public Office Commission. The only argument advanced against it is the insistence on the innocence of Irish corporate culture by the Company Law Review Group. Yet in this case, who dares to be most fatuous wins. It is long since time that those disclosing legal or ethical concerns in good faith should know that they will be listened to and protected from retaliation.

These changes in the political and business culture could create a genuine shift in attitudes, in which the amoral minority no longer sets the standards and the decent majority is no longer intimidated into silence. But change at the top will not be sustained unless it reflects the adoption by Irish society as a whole of a new public morality.

There has to be a belief that enough is enough – both in the sense of no longer being willing to put up with a system that has done so much harm and in the sense of moving towards a society that can give everyone enough to enjoy the dignity of citizenship.

There has to be a whole new kind of intolerance – not for those who are merely different, but for greed, cynicism and the pursuit of private gain at the expense of the public good. There has to be a new sense of national pride – not the weepy sentimentality of pub patriotism or the wilful self-delusion of those who cannot acknowledge the state we're in, but a belief in our collective capacity to create a country to be proud of. There has to be a new kind of confidence – not the hollow reassurance that a return to the boom years is just around the corner, but a sober awareness that a much better society is within our grasp.

There has to a new kind of individualism – not the rugged cowboy ethic of doing whatever you can get away with, but the idea of taking personal responsibility for the public realm. There has to be a new kind of collectivism – not the tribal and parochial loyalties that have shaped the political culture, but a wider sense of mutual obligation. There has to be a new notion of austerity – not as an attack on the soft targets of those who have least but as a revulsion for excess, waste and well-rewarded fecklessness. There has to be a new idea of the republic, not as an end which will be achieved at some mythical point in the future, but as a beginning, a set of conditions in which people are given the chance to live with dignity. In the second decade of the twentieth century, many Irish people decided that a republic was worth dying for. In the second decade of the twenty-first century, many more can decide that a republic is worth living in.

Fifty Ideas for Action

This is a summary of the immediate actions recommended in the course of this book.

It may surprise some readers that there has been no direct discussion of a subject much debated when the question of political reform has been raised – changing the 1937 constitution. Support for the current constitution is low. An *Irish Times* poll in September 2010 found just 12 per cent of respondents agreeing that it has 'stood the test of time well', with 59 per cent believing it needs some amendment and 19 per cent suggesting that it needs to be entirely rewritten.

It is obvious from everything that has been written here that I agree with the sentiments of the large majority who want constitutional change. I do not, however, believe that we should start the debate about political transformation with a discussion about the constitution, which would quickly get bogged down in legal and abstract issues. Rather, the way we change the constitution should be a function of what it is we decide we want to do with our society and our political system. We needs to be clear about what kind of political entity it is to be the constitution *of*.

Large-scale constitutional change is certainly necessary to enable many of the key transformations I suggest here: to establish powerful local government; to change the voting system for national elections; to establish real accountability of governments to parliament; to renovate or abolish the Seanad; to enable the Oireachtas to conduct meaningful inquiries; to clarify the right to freedom of conscience; and to make clear once and for all that the rights of private property do not outweigh the common good. It is also fairly obvious that I believe that much of the religious rhetoric in the constitution is damaging to both religion and politics. It is part of the legacy of 1930s Ireland that has been petrified within the constitution (the representation of the role of women is another part), and that needs to be cut away. It is also obvious that I believe that the Democratic Programme of the First Dáil would be a much better place to go in search of first principles of republicanism. Agreement on these goals, however, should determine constitutional change, not the other way around.

Fifty Key Actions

1 Establish an effective system of local democracy, with tax-raising powers and significant control over large aspects of education, health, policing and other public services. Make clear links between local taxes and local spending.

2 Transfer the useful functions of quangos to local councils unless there is a compelling case for doing otherwise.

3 Rationalise local councils so that each voter has broadly the same level of representation.

4 Ban councillors from working as auctioneers, property developers or property or planning consultants.

5 Bring in legally binding national standards for planning

and development and give the National Spatial Strategy statutory status.

6 Implement the Kenny report of 1974, allowing councils to purchase development land for its existing value plus 25 per cent.

7 Establish 'deliberative democracy' experiments in every substantial community in tandem with new local government structures.

8 Severely limit the ability of governments to use the 'guillotine' mechanism to pass legislation that has not been debated in parliament.

9 Oblige ministers to release the full files that are prepared for draft answers to parliamentary questions.

10 End the fiction that ministers are responsible for everything that happens in their departments. Make them responsible for decisions they take and for information they ought to know. Make senior civil servants responsible for the decisions they take.

11 Restore and strengthen the right of the Oireachtas to carry out inquiries into all decisions made by public bodies and all activities involving the use of public money. Give parliamentary committees the same powers of compellability as those enjoyed by tribunals of inquiry.

12 Make all appointments to state and public boards open to public competition and subject to Oireachtas scrutiny.

13 Reduce the size of the Dáil to 100 members.

14 Either make the Seanad representative of civil society, social partners and the new local councils within a short time frame, or abolish it.

15 Change the Dáil electoral system to the additional member system.

16 Introduce a gender quota of at least 30 per cent, to be

enforced by reducing public payments to political parties by the degree to which they fail to introduce gender
balance.

17 Apply equality laws to religious-owned institutions,
outlawing discrimination against teachers and health
workers on grounds of religion or sexuality. End the
discriminatory practices which prevent non-Christians
from training as primary teachers.

18 Hand primary schools over to local and democratic
ownership and control. Make them non-sectarian, with
provision for religious education outside of the core
curriculum.

19 Replace GDP as the primary measure of progress with
a well-being index along the lines developed by Joseph
Stiglitz, Amartya Sen and Jean Paul Fitoussi.

20 Radically curtail tax incentives for private pensions and
stop putting money into the National Pension Reserve
Fund. Use the money instead to increase the state
pension for everyone to 40 per cent of pre-retirement
income. Top this up to 50 per cent through a Social
Insurance Retirement Fund.

21 End all property-related tax breaks.

22 Conduct a rigorous audit of vacant housing estates
to determine which can realistically be used for social
housing.

23 Adopt a long-term national goal of pegging house
prices in Ireland to Western European averages.

24 Switch spending from both social welfare rent supplements paid to private landlords and tax breaks for landlords to the provision of decent social housing.

25 Introduce a national system of Social Health Insurance,
abolishing the two-tier health system. Adopt the

principle of 'access on the basis of need; payment on the basis of income'.

26 Radically reduce the size of the Health Service Executive.

27 Switch more health spending towards community and preventive services. Implement the primary care strategy.

28 Increase the number of GPs to European levels.

29 Accept the need to spend more money on education as an absolute necessity for social justice and economic development.

30 End subsidies for private second-level schools.

31 Charge university fees to those who can afford them. Increase grants for those who are currently excluded.

32 Expand adult and continuing education. Consider the idea of individual 'education funds' attaching equally to each citizen.

33 Identify children at risk of failure from an early age and intervene immediately with personal and family supports.

34 Adopt an active policy of reducing the gap between the highest and lowest earners. Make the pay of those at the top a fixed percentage of that of those at the bottom.

35 Resist attempts to cut the minimum wage.

36 Bring general levels of taxation up to average European levels.

37 Create a fair tax system by reducing tax breaks to average EU levels, saving over €5 billion.

38 Employ 500 unemployed finance workers on two-year contracts to conduct tax audits.

39 Introduce a property tax to help fund local government.

40 Limit the number of directorships of public companies that any one individual can hold at the same time to three.

41 Give coherent legislative protection to bona fide whistleblowers.

42 Restore the Freedom of Information Act to its former status

43 Create a register of lobbyists and publish records of all meetings between lobbyists, ministers and public officials.

44 Ban ministers and senior civil servants from working as lobbyists for at least three years after they leave office.

45 Change the remit of the Company Law Review Group from the current one of encouraging industry to one of preventing white-collar crime. Conduct a thorough review of Irish company law to determine why white-collar crime is still likely to go unpunished.

46 Widen the obligations of auditors to report reckless as well as illegal behaviour.

47 Replace the current ineffective Ethics in Public Office Act with a new, unified and clear code of ethics for the holders of all public offices. Strengthen the definition of a 'connected' person to include anyone who has a material interest at stake.

48 Ban all significant private donations to political parties.

49 Force all registered parties to publish full annual accounts.

50 Declare a republic.

Notes

INTRODUCTION: The Wrong Map

1 Thomas Murphy, *The Gigli Concert*, Gallery Books, Dublin, 1984.
2 *Irish Times*, 24 October 2008.
3 *New York Times*, 2 September 2010.
4 *Financial Times*, 12 September 2010.
5 *The Irish Banking Crisis: Regulatory and Financial Stability Policy 2003–2008*, A Report to the Minister for Finance by the Governor of the Central Bank, 2010.

PART ONE: FIVE MYTHS
   1 The Myth of the Republic

1 *Dáil Eireann Debates*, Vol. 1, 21 January 1919.
2 *Commission to Inquire into Child Abuse*, 2009, Vol. 1, chapter 3.
3 G. W. Russell, *Co-operation and Nationality*, Maunsel, Dublin, 1912.
4 Arthur Mitchell and Padraig O Snodaigh (eds.), *Irish Political Documents 1916–1949*, Irish Academic Press, 1985.
5 Philip Pettit, *Republicanism: A Theory of Freedom and Government*, Oxford University Press, 1997.
6 Both quotes are from Louise Fuller, *Irish Catholicism since 1950*, Gill and Macmillan, Dublin, 2002.
7 Mary Kenny, *Crown and Shamrock*, New Island, Dublin, 2009.
8 Seanad debates, 12 March 2003.

   2 The Myth of Representation

1 *Irish Times*, 13 April 2002.

2 *Irish Times*, 16 January 2007.
3 *Irish Independent*, 19 August 2008.
4 Lee Komito, 'Irish Clientelism: A Reappraisal', *The Economic and Social Review*, Vol. 15. No. 3, April 1984.
5 Oireachtas Joint Committee on the Constitution, Third Interim Report, February 2010.
6 In 32 *Counties: Photographs of Ireland* by Donovan Wylie, Secker and Warburg, London, 1989.
7 Deiric O'Broin and Eugene Waters, *Governing Below the Centre: Local Governance in Ireland*, tasc@New Island, Dublin, 2007
8 Diarmaid Ferriter, *Lovers of Liberty?: Local Government in 20th Century Ireland*, National Archives of Ireland, Dublin, 2001
9 Paula Clancy and Grainne Murphy, *Outsourcing Government: Public Bodies and Accountability*, tasc@New Island, Dublin, 2006.
10 *Irish Examiner*, 12 June 2010.
11 James Nix, paper at the Irish Planning Institute conference, April 2010.
12 National Institute for Regional and Spatial Analysis, *A Haunted Landscape: Housing and Ghost Estates in Post-Celtic Tiger Ireland*, Maynooth, July 2010.

3 The Myth of Parliamentary Democracy

1 Office of the Ombudsman, *Report on Nursing Home Subventions*, January 2001.
2 Sean Dooney and John O'Toole, *Irish Government Today*, Gill and Macmillan, Dublin, 1992.
3 Eamon Delaney, *An Accidental Diplomat*, New Island, Dublin, 2001
4 Muiris MacCarthaigh, *Accountability in Irish Parliamentary Politics*, Institute of Public Administration, Dublin, 2005.
5 Dáil debates, 1 November 1989.
6 Oireachtas Joint Committee on Health and Children, 21 April 2005.
7 Address to the Burren Law School, 2 May 2010.
8 Maguire *v*. Ardagh, Supreme Court, 2002.
9 *Irish Times*, 2 August 2010.
10 *Irish Times*, 23 July 2010.

11 Clodagh Harris (ed.), *Report of the Democracy Commission*, Tasc@New Island, 2005.

12 *Irish Times*, 4 August 2010.

4 The Myth of Charity

1 See Donald Harman Akenson, *A Mirror to Kathleen's Face: Education in Independent Ireland 1922–1960*, McGill-Queen's University Press, Montreal and London, 1975.

2 Barry Coldrey, *Faith and Fatherland: The Christian Brothers and the Development of Irish Nationalism, 1838–1921*, Gill and Macmillan, Dublin, 1988.

3 Tom Inglis, *Moral Monopoly: The Rise and Fall of the Catholic Church in Modern Ireland*, University College Dublin Press, 1998.

4 John McGahern, *Memoir*, Faber and Faber, London, 2005.

5 Ruth Barrington, *Health, Medicine and Politics in Ireland 1900–1970*, Institute of Public Administration, Dublin, 1987.

6 James H. Moynihan, *The Life of Archbishop John Ireland*, Harper, New York, 1953.

7 *Irish Times*, 5 April 2010

8 *Irish Times*, 25 January 2010

5 The Myth of Wealth

1 *Irish Independent*, 9 September 2002.

2 Forfás, *National Competitiveness Report*, 2010.

3 Davy Research, *Irish Macro Comment*, 19 February 2010.

4 Bank of Ireland Private Banking, *The Wealth of the Nation*, 2007.

5 John Kelly, Mary Cussen and Gillian Phelan, *The Net Worth of Irish Households: An Update*, Central Bank, 2007.

6 Forfás, *A Baseline Assessment of Ireland's Oil Dependence*, April 2006.

7 Sustainable Energy Ireland, Renewable Energy in Ireland, 2010 update.

8 *Meath Chronicle*, 3 February 2010.

9 *Irish Times*, 17 November 2008.

10 *Irish Independent*, 29 June 2009.

11 *Irish Times*, 15 June 2005 and 25 June 2010.

12 *Irish Independent*, 25 January 2008.

13 Commission of the European Communities, *Implementation of the Barcelona Objectives Concerning Childcare Facilities*, October 2008.

14 Health Insurance Authority, *Competition in the Irish Health Insurance Market*, 2007.

15 *Irish Times*, 29 February 2008.

16 Michael Punch, *The Irish Housing System*, Jesuit Centre for Faith and Justice, 2009.

17 Oireachtas Joint Committee on Social Protection, 29 April 2009.

18 Colin Crouch, *After Privatised Keynesianism*, Compass, November 2008 (compassonline.org.uk).

19 Report of the Commission on the Measurement of Economic Performance and Social Progress, www.stiglitz-sen-fitoussi.fr.

20 The Great Transition, www.neweconomics.org.

PART TWO: FIVE DECENCIES

  1 Gimme Shelter: The Decency of Security

1 OECD, *Pensions at a Glance*, 2009.

2 Rubicon Investment Consulting, Group Pension Managed Funds Update to 31 July 2010.

3 National Pension Reserve Fund, Annual Report 2009.

4 Jim Stewart, presentation at Kilkenny Arts Festival, 11 August 2010.

5 TASC, *Making Pensions Work for People*, January 2010.

6 OECD, *Society at a Glance: 2009 social indicators*.

7 National Pensions Framework Document, 2010.

8 National Pensions Board, Annual Report, 2009.

9 Teresa Ghillarducci, *When I'm Sixty-Four: The Plot Against Pensions and the Plan to Save Them*, Princeton University Press, 2008.

10 Gerard Hughes, *Executive Directors' Pensions 2008*, TCD Pension Policy Research Group.

11 *Irish Times*, 25 September 2009.

12 Michael Punch, *The Irish Housing System: Vision, Values, Reality*, The Jesuit Centre for Faith and Justice, 2009.

13 Dermot Coates and Naomi Feely, *Promoting Improved Standards in the Private Rented Sector: Review of Policy and Practice*, Centre for Housing Research, November 2007.

14 P. J. Drudy and Michael Punch, *Out of Reach: Inequalities in the Irish Housing System,* tasc@ New Island, Dublin, 2005.

15 *Irish Times,* 14 October 1999.

16 National Institute for Regional and Spatial Analysis, *A Haunted Landscape: Housing and Ghost Estates in Post-Celtic Tiger Ireland,* July 2010.

17 Department of the Environment, *Interim Value for Money and Policy Review of the Rental Accommodation Scheme* (RAS), October 2009; Department of Social Protection press release, 10 June 2010.

18 Focus Ireland, *Building Homes, Creating Jobs, Stimulating the Economy,* Pre-Budget Submission, 2008.

19 Minister for Finance, Dáil questions, 3 November 2009.

20 Eithne Fitzgerald and Nessa Winston, 'Housing, Equality and Inequality', in Michelle Norris and Declan Redmond (eds), *Housing Contemporary Ireland,* Institute of Public Administration, Dublin, 2005.

21 *Irish Independent,* 8 September 2006; *Irish Times,* 23 April 2009.

2 Beyond the Sickness System: The Decency of Health

1 OECD, Health Data 2010.

2 Department of Health and Children, *Health in Ireland: Key Trends,* 2009.

3 Department of Health and Children, *Submission to the Commission on Taxation,* 2009.

4 Public Health Alliance, *Health Inequalities on the Island of Ireland,* 2007.

5 A. McCarthy and P. Kirke, 'Absolute and Socioeconomically Stratified Trends in Birth Rate and Infant Mortality Rate in Ireland 1984–2005', *Irish Journal of Medical Science,* forthcoming.

6 C. Farrell, H. McAvoy, J. Wilde and Combat Poverty Agency, *Tackling Health Inequalities: An All-Ireland Approach to Social Determinants,* Dublin, Combat Poverty Agency/Institute of Public Health in Ireland, 2008, and European Commission, *Economic Implications of Socio-economic Inequalities in Health in the European Union,* July 2007.

7 *Irish Times,* 26 July 2010.

8 Department of Health and Children, *Report of the Expert Group*

on Resource Allocation and Financing in the Health Sector, July
2010.

9 Dr Philip Crowley, *Health Inequalities and General Practice in
Deprived Areas*, Combat Poverty Research Seminar, January 2006.

10 *Irish Times*, 5 January 2010.

11 *British Medical Journal*, 11 August 2010.

12 *Irish Times*, 11 February 2009.

13 Irish Heart Foundation, *National Audit of Stroke Care*, April
2008.

14 Oireachtas Joint Committee on Health and Children, *Report on
Primary Medical Care in the Community*, February 2010

15 The Adelaide Hospital Society reports are prepared by the TCD
Centre for Health Policy and Management and written by Stephen
Thomas, Padhraig Ryan and Charles Normand. They are: *Effec-
tive Foundations for the Financing and Organisation of SHI in
Ireland; Universal Health Insurance: The Way Forward for Irish
Healthcare; Social Health Insurance: Further Options for Ireland*
and *Social Health Insurance: Options for Ireland*, 2006–10.

16 TCD Centre for Health Policy and Management, *There's No
Place Like Home: A Cost and Outcomes Analysis of Alternative
Models of Care for Young Children with Severe Disabilities in
Ireland*, February 2010

3 A Smart Society: The Decency of Education

1 Growing Up in Ireland, *Child Cohort, Key Findings: The Education of 9-Year-Olds*, November 2009.

2 James Williams and Sheila Greene, 'Key Outcomes for Children:
New Evidence from Growing Up in Ireland', *ESRI Quarterly
Economic Commentary*, April 2010.

3 CSO, SILC 2008.

4 Higher Education Authority, *National Plan for Equity of Access
to Higher Education 2008–2013*.

5 Irish Times, 15 August 2008.

6 National Competitiveness Council, *Statement on Education and
Training*, 2009.

7 Unicef, Report Card 8, *The Childcare Transition*, 2008.

8 OECD, *The High Cost of Low Educational Performance*, 2010.

4 Beyond the Ultimatum Game: The Decency of Equality

1 Pete Lunn, *Basic Instincts: Human Nature and the New Economics*, Marshall Cavendish, London, 2008.
2 *The Solidarity Factor: Responses to Economic Inequality in Ireland*, Tasc, August 2010.
3 CSO, SILC 2008.
4 OECD, *Growing Unequal: Income Distribution and Poverty in OECD Countries*, 2008.
5 *Irish Times*, 23 April 2008.
6 Paula Clancy, Nat O'Connor and Kevin Dillon, *Mapping the Golden Circle*, Tasc, May 2010.
7 Remarks by Angel Gurría, OECD Secretary-General, Paris, 21 October 2008.
8 Howard Gardner, *Frames of Mind: The Theory of Multiple Intelligences*, Basic Books, New York, 2003.
9 Daniel Dorling, *Injustice: Why Social Inequality Persists*, Policy Press, Bristol, 2010.
10 *Irish Times*, 21 April 2010.
11 *Irish Times*, 28 August 2010.
12 Revenue Commissioners, *Analysis of High Income Individuals' Restriction 2008*, July 2010.
13 *Irish Times*, 28 August 2010.
14 Social Justice Ireland, *An Agenda for a New Ireland*, 2010.
15 Ronan Lyons, www.ronanlyons.com/2009/04/07.

5 Ethical Austerity: The Decency of Citizenship

1 Tony Judt, 'Austerity', *New York Review of Books*, 13 May 2010.
2 Michael Fogarty, Liam Ryan and Joseph Lee (eds), *Irish Values and Attitudes*, Dominican Publications, Dublin, 1984.
3 Patrick Honohan et al., *The Banking Crisis in Ireland: Regulatory and Financial Stability*, June 2010.
4 *Irish Times*, 23 January 2010.
5 Company Law Review Group, Annual Report 2007.
6 Ernst and Young, *Driving Ethical Growth: New Markets, New Challenges*, 11th Global Fraud Survey, 2010.
7 Standards in Public Office Commission, Annual Report, 2009.
8 *Irish Times*, 6 March 2010.

Index

DIRT (Deposit Interest Retention Tax) scandal, 73, 81, 210, 218, 221, 222
Dorling, Daniel, 201
Drudy, P. J., 146

Economist, 112
education, 85–92, 98–106, 108–10, 122–3, 177–91, 243; infrastructure, 119
Education Act, 100
Electoral Act, 35, 36, 230
electoral systems, 78–80
emigration, 5–6
Employment Equality Act, 101, 105
Enright, Olwyn, 76
Ethics in Public Office Act, 35, 244
EU (European Union) statistical comparisons, 114, 121, 135–6, 163, 168, 170, 181, 195, 203, 208

Fahey, Denis, 92
Fianna Fáil, 4, 13, 14–15, 21, 49–50, 147, 156, 218, 228, 231
Financial Services Regulatory Authority, 219
Financial Times, 9, 10
Fine Gael, 198, 231
Fingleton, Michael, 15, 142, 198, 200
Finneran, Michael, 61–2
Fitoussi, Jean Paul, 126, 242
FitzGerald, Niall, 234
FitzPatrick, Seán, 15, 196–7, 200
Flavin, Jim, 225

Flynn, Eileen, 100–1
Foley, Denis, 35
Freedom of Information Act, 35, 227, 244

Gardner, Howard, 201
GDP, as inaccurate measure of national wealth, 113–16, 125–6, 242
Ghilarducci, Teresa, 141
Gormley, John, 227
Greene, Sheila, 177–8
Growing Up in Ireland, 177, 188
'guillotine' system, 63–5, 241
Gurría, Angel, 200–1
Guth, Werner, 192

Hanafin, Mary, 228
Harney, Mary, 200
Haughey, Charles, 4, 30
healthcare, 159–176; primary care strategy, 171–2, 175, 243; spending, 159
health insurance, 121–2, 160-1, 173–4, 242–3
Health Service Executive (HSE), 51–2, 142, 161, 163–4, 175, 243
Healey-Rea, Jackie, 43
Heraty, Ann, 196–7
Holub, Miroslav, 2
Honohan, Patrick, 14–16, 218
housing, 145–58; construction boom, 53, 115–16, 123, 145, 148
hospitals, 119–20, 164–8
Howley, Ian, 122
Hughes, Gerard, 139, 141–2